I0796464

COMMENTRIES
ON
SRI AUROBINDO'S THOUGHT

COMMENTARIES
ON
SRI AUROBINDO'S THOUGHT

M. P. PANDIT

1

First Published in 1988
Reprinted 1995

Published by :

Dipti Publications
Sri Aurobindo Ashram
Pondicherry, India

Printed at : All India Press, Kennedy Nagar,
P.O. Box - 51, Pondicherry - 605 001.

CONTENTS

"BEAUTIFUL ROSE: SRI AUROBINDO"

Sri Aurobindo was a revolutionary through and through. To whichever field he turned, he broke away from old traditions and opened the horizons for fresh departures. Even as a small boy in England, he had visions of vast changes coming over the world presaging a new order in the life-movement and he was impelled to prepare himself to participate in the gathering movements. He spearheaded a move to promote a revolution for the liberation of India to begin with. He followed it up, on his return to India at the age of 21, with an intensive campaign to turn the prevalent mentality of petition and prayer into a powerful surge of a countrywide revolution—not only political but even military. He sounded the battle-cry of Bande Mataram through his writings that spread fire over all the land and, side by side, organised an underground movement of militant opposition to the British rule. He was to continue to work for the freedom of the country all his life, though his means changed. And he had the satisfaction of seeing the dawn of freedom for India on his birthday, August 15, 1947.

As part of his efforts to recast the life of his countrymen in freer mould truer to the genius of the Indian people, he set afoot a strong movement to introduce a *national education* based upon psychological perceptions that had inspired the Indian mind down the ages till the Western impact brought in an alien note of utilitarianism and commercialism. The Sri Aurobindo International Centre of Education in his Ashram continues the work initiated by him to new-base the whole system of education on aesthetic and soul-values. He blazed a new trail in meeting the challenge of life. All along the religious and spiritual tradition in India—and indeed all over the world—had been other-worldly. Life on earth had been devalued and the solution envisaged elsewhere, in some Beyond—a paradise or a Nihil. Sri Aurobindo was a pioneer in departing from this established approach and calling for acceptance of life with a view to changing and perfecting it, instead of running away from it. To this end, he worked upon and built his philosophy of *The Life Divine*, bridging the gulf between Spirit and Matter, God and the World. In the place of one-sided readings of the cosmic movement, he presented an integral perspective which embraced the entire gamut of life—and sub-life—and traced its growth in a mighty movement of evolution of Consciousness towards some ultimate perfection. He restored dignity to Man and placed him on the crest of the advancing wave of evolutionary progression and foresaw his eventual transmutation into a divine man shaping a world of harmony, unity and peace. In his approach Science and Spirituality, Nature and God, the Individual and the Society, the nation and humanity—all meet in a happy collaboration to fulfil the creative Intention which is to manifest the Kingdom of God on Earth.

He was not content with merely erecting a masterly philosophical edifice. He perfected the Path to translate this Vision into practice and worked to make it coextensive with life in the world. His is the Integral Yoga which combines the best features of all the traditional yogas, the Tantra and the Veda, metapsychology of consciousness. In simple terms, his is a holistic discipline that covers all the different parts of the human being—the physical, the vital, the mental, the emotional, the psychic and the spiritual. It gathers up the whole being and nature of man into a combined movement of concentration and expansion, deepening and heightening, and above all integrating the personality around the divine core at the centre. It aims at a triple transformation of human nature—psychic, spiritual and supramental. It combines three dimensions of creation in man: the individual, the universal and the transcendental. And what is most significant of this discipline is that it takes up life with all its diverse elements for change and elevation. Life becomes an opportunity to grow, to fulfil. This is a revolution that touches every man in every walk of life, at every point.

Sri Aurobindo is recorded to have been a voracious reader in his younger days. His interests were history, literature, languages—all that dealt with the life of the peoples of all ages, all races, not so much their philosophies or metaphysics dealing with airier subjects. But it is not so well known that he was a great writer, to whom no subject was taboo, no theme too light for high treatment. Politics, Polity, Social Sciences, Dramas and Plays, Lyrics and Narratives, Sonnets and Short Stories, Literary Criticism, Creative Surveys of Cultures, Insights into ancient scriptures—all these and many more were the themes covered in the thousands of pages of his works. And yet, none of these were products of his intellect. His mind was absolutely silent when the writings flowed directly into his pen! But that is another story. Suffice it to note that all that he wrote is essentially creative, opening new horizons. Recently I was told by an eminent authority on English literature that Sri Aurobindo's work, 'Future Poetry', tracing the course of English poetry down the centuries and predicting the lines on which it is likely to develop in future, has come in for great appreciation in a far-off country like Australia though, lamentably, our own critics obstinately refuse to look at it. So too Sri Aurobindo's epic *Savitri*, which is a mantric utterance *par excellance*, running into 24 thousand lines of evocatory poetry. The theme is derived in outline from the old legend of Savitri-Satyavan, but the form it has taken at the hands of this master-seer is totally new. It has a rare power, beauty of sound and imagery; its pinnacled structure has many storeys: history, occultism, philosophy, psychology, cosmology, symbolism, spiritual experience. It is the Veda of the future. Naturally there is a resistance to it in quarters that seek to stick to lowland plains or luxuriate in the grotesque. But it is rapidly gaining ground in the higher mind of humanity. Being his last testament to humanity it is also a charter for the superhumanity to come.

And then there is of course his mighty work in the spiritual field which is necessarily unseen by the public eye, but nevertheless testified to by those heroic spirits who are engaged in their incessant quest of the high peaks of Supreme Reality. New ways have been opened, new heights scaled and age-long barriers broken by the intense labours of the Seer of the Supramental Truth in his mission to assure for the Earth-Mother a life of error-free truth, evil-free good, strife-free peace and harmony.

Beauty, say the rhetors of India's aesthetics, is what is ever new, fresh at every moment. Sri Aurobindo's personality and work have a perpetual relevance; they have always something new to look to. Love for all orders of creation flows out from every feeling, every word, every act of this pragmatic mystic. And Love is symbolised by the purple Rose.

Humanity salutes the BEAUTIFUL ROSE.

5-12-1987 (*Courtesy: All India Radio*)

COMMENTARIES

1

LOVE IN HUMAN RELATIONS

It is a common notion that for spiritual life love for humans is a snare. It is reputed to entangle the person in attachments and keep him in the net of maya. Hence the injunction, beware of human emotions. They are part of the mechanism of lower nature, *prakriti* to keep you fettered.

The consequences of this doctrine have been deleterious. A deliberate effort is made to dry up the emotions and refuse to participate in human relationships. As a result all tender and soft feelings, sympathy, affection, are suppressed and denied. The result is that one loses the zest for life and develops a cold and insensitive nature which borders on cruelty, callousness.

But this hardening of nature is usually found to operate only where others are concerned. Closing himself from meaningful interchange with others, man tends to be centred around himself. He becomes his sole concern, the object of his interests. He becomes insufferably egoistic and considers himself to be superior to the common folk who are deluded by enslaving emotions. Self-righteous, he becomes a prisoner of asceticism and turns his back upon the Beauty and Joy aspects of the Divine in manifestation. In the long run he is the loser. He stunts half his growth and acts as a damper on the environment. He develops a perverse taste for barrenness, ugliness, denial of life. Negation is his philosophy of life.

He misses a golden opportunity of growing into God, embracing his creation and proceeding through life-experience at its fullest, to his intended fulfilment in which all stands justified, everything becomes a stepping stone—including human relationships, human love and sympathy.

2

HUMAN LOVE AND DIVINE LOVE

When we speak of human relationships as stepping stones to divine Love, we naturally have in mind a love that is human but not vitiated by physical desire or the vital spirit of possession. A movement that is so physical and vital may be natural at a crude, primitive stage of evolution but it is certainly not contributive to the possibility of higher love. Still, even in human love which starts with a genuine note, there is a psychic vibration which if tended and nourished can definitely lead to a pure and divine movement. Such love has a deeper origin though later on it may acquire a vital coating. As long as it has the psychic element and keeps link with its source in the psychic, this love is elevating, purifying. Its first expression is self-giving. One gives oneself more and more to the object of love. One gives without regard to whether it is recognised or responded to. This is the first exercise in breaking out of the prison of vital ego which always wants to take and possess. Once this movement to surrender oneself—no matter to whom and to what—starts, it is easier to surrender to the Divine when one is pulled in that direction.

Adoration is an important part of such healthy love. In the act of adoration the ego thins out and one finds oneself spontaneously by growing in the image of the beloved. This has important possibilities in the context of love for the Divine. It pushes relentlessly toward the destination of union with the loved. Of course it is not physical union that is meant—though poets like Blake would describe the physical act of love as part of divine love fulfilling itself. Whatever the truth of the matter, it is a fact that if there be a psychic or even a truer element in human love, it does contribute to the evolution of the person.

Thus it is no part of spiritual life to shun and shut out human love. It must be used as a spring-board to soar into a higher dimension. Naturally one must be careful to reject movements of desire, sense of possession, claim, developments that inevitably tend to enter and dig themselves in under the specious plea of love. Love should be saved from the danger of attachment. Sri Aurobindo observes that attachment is egoism in love. The personal factor in the human situation must be eliminated. That is a good exercise preparing for the spiritual consummation of utter surrender to the Divine: the person melts.

3

PREPARATORY ROLE OF LOVE

Love always draws from the deeper springs of life. He who loves or begins to love becomes more and more aware of his emotions, movements below the surface being. He forgets himself, his little ego-bound, self-centred person, and allows himself to be claimed by a larger movement of self-giving, abandon. During such movements he experiences a double change in consciousness: he expands, he touches some deeper levels of his being which exude warmth, tenderness and purity. This prepares the way for an awakening of the Divinity within. His nature undergoes a pleasant elevation. The psychic element gets a chance to come to the front and lend its character to the love-movement.

It is possible that instead of the psychic factor it is the higher vital that takes over. This higher vital is not vitiated by desire and attachment which are the hall-mark of the lower vital; it is expansive, fiery and spreads itself spontaneously. Love under its spell tends to acquire a universal character. It becomes dynamic and exults in flowing out on all. The seeker must take care not to confuse this with the psychic.

The psychic gives depth, is gentle and pure. It does not insist on being accepted or react on being not recognised. It exists and flows for itself. There is no agitation, no compulsive sense of mission about it. It is only concerned with imparting its divine character to the love that is sprouting. Love gives a much needed opportunity to the psychic to come to the front and participate in the evolution of the person's nature. Through love crude nature learns to shed its grossness and become a fit instrument for the radiation of the soul within, directly and indirectly.

4

OPENING TO THE PSYCHIC

We spoke of the psychic. The psychic, as we know, is the divine essence in each being. It is the soul which is involved in the movement of evolution unlike the self which is not involved but supports the evolutionary movement from its immutable status behind. If the self is termed Atman, the psychic may be described as *antarātman*, projection of the self within the movement as the soul. This psychic is our direct link with the Divine and the source of all impulsions towards the Divine and all qualities and modes that lead to the Divine. Much of the labour in yoga for the Divine is lightened if we can open to the psychic and let it act in moulding our nature and developing our consciousness. How do we do that?

It goes without saying that there has to be change in our daily pattern of life. Movements that are inconsistent with the demands of psychic verities like truth, purity, harmony, joy, love, must be rigorously eschewed. Those that build these elements in our life must be promoted. This is what is called building the climate of the psychic. Besides this general orientation, there are certain techniques in yogic discipline that Sri Aurobindo mentions.

To make the mind quiet. Normally the mind is full of restless activity, jumping from thought to thought, so much so that some even confuse mind with thought. Thinking is only one activity of the mind. Apart from thoughts there are sensations of all kinds, eagerness, fear etc. There are flights of imagination, fantasies. All in all, the mind is always occupied with one thing or other and along with the mind we are lost in its incessant rounds. This uncontrolled activity of the mind must be checked and the mind stabilised into a quieter state. Then alone can our deeper elements like the psychic get an opportunity to send up their intimations to the surface. It is only in silence that the psychic can be felt and its direction received. Whether by practice of meditation or concentration, the mind must be controlled, disciplined and quieted into a habitual calm.

Or, the mind must be educated to withdraw from its customary preoccupations with purely mundane interests—without and within—and turn towards the Divine. Once the mind starts taking interest in things leading to the Divine, it learns to dwell on the higher or deeper aspects of existence. And if it so wills, it can impose its choice upon the rest of the being. An opening is created for the psychic to extend its influence and participate in the life-movement.

Still another way is to separate the purusha from the prakriti. We learn to disassociate ourselves from the routine movements of our nature and hold back our consciousness in a witness position. Activity goes on—and has to go on in a substantial measure—but we do not identify ourselves with it. We treat it as mechanical movements of nature and we stand back as observers to begin with. This gives a release to our being from helpless involvement in the gyrations of nature. And in this status there is an effortless opening to the soul within. It is understood that a strong will and ceaseless vigilance are needed for this purpose. But if we are earnest about it it is not as difficult as it may appear. The difficult part in this discipline is at the beginning: to effect a breakthrough. Once a separation is effected, the rest follows. We have only to remain unmoved in our detached position.

5

CLOUDING OF THE PSYCHIC

Opening to the psychic is not a one-time affair. Once there is an opening, the communication must be naturalised. Care is to be taken to ensure that other messages are not allowed to interfere or overlay the psychic intimations. For there are in us several sources of misguidance. Every voice is not the voice of the soul. More often than not it is the voice of the desire-ego, the vital usurper, a mental preference, a deliberate misguidance by the Enemy. Again, voice is not the only way of communication. In fact in view of the facility with which pseudo-voices crowd out the genuine one, the seeker is even advised not to trust to any voice.

The psychic has its own ways of communication. It makes itself felt as a strong impulse from the heart region. Its intimation may reach the surface in the form of a special feeling: this feeling comes from the depths, carries an authenticity about it and makes itself clear without any ambiguity about it. But it is not insistent. It does not force itself with vehemence like a vital suggestion. It is a quiet, firm, direction.

This intimation is precious. It should be looked for and cherished. Quite often the vital throws a wet blanket over it if it be contrary to its own choice, the mind raises a doubt under the influence of the vital or its own preference. And it is possible that one ignores the inner intimation. The psychic is not discouraged, it repeats a few times. If it is still passed over—as often happens when one is set on a different course—it recedes and waits for a time when the being is more ready. The psychic is pushed back, it is clouded.

This is an ever-present danger against which the sadhaka has to guard himself. Whenever the inner direction is found to be contrary to what the mind persuades itself as the right course, it is time to pause and look into oneself more attentively. Nature in ignorance has several ways of off-setting the choice of the soul. One may brush aside the question raised from within; one may advance specious reasons why it should be dismissed; one may know in one's enlightened part that it is right but if the will is weak, one may be stampeded along the pleasanter course. In all cases the psychic feels denied and if this happens more often, it feels defeated and retires into its secrecy.

A constant vigilance is necessary. And what is more, a minimum of honesty must be there. One must have the courage to accept and work out the directive from within despite temptations to smother the inconvenient voice of the soul and ride on the drive of the vital.

The psychic does not demand, it does not impose itself. It has a certain sadness when it is consistently ignored. This makes itself felt in the being as an uneasiness, some out-of-sorts feeling, some sense of loss. That is the time to beware and correct oneself. If the habit of listening to the psychic is sincerely cultivated and made natural, all is smooth sailing. If it is not taken notice of due to ignorance, the way to set things right is still open. But if it is deliberately set aside, ignored, it is a betrayal of the psychic which then withdraws into its shell. Much labour is needed before it can be persuaded to emerge once again into the open.

6

PHYSICAL CONSCIOUSNESS

Just as we have a mental consciousness and a vital consciousness, we have too a physical consciousness. This consciousness includes the body-consciousness and relates to the physical aspect of our existence—physical desires, physical needs, physical habits etc. The mind functions, more or less, on the principle of the intellect in its several operations; the vital is governed largely by desire, movement to effectuate itself; the physical has for its basic principle, a fixed stability, inertia, solidity. Based as they are on the foundation of physical matter, both the vital and the mind are subject to the pull of the physical. This consciousness always holds back the movement and flight of the other two. In a sense this immobility is its virtue. Nature has deliberately built this bastion of stability in this world of flux. But it also works as a handicap. Especially in efforts to change our nature, to go beyond the hold of material nature, this consciousness proves an almost insuperable obstacle. It has an obstinate, repetitive nature which refuses to leave the old moorings and accept new positions. It always harks back and asserts its primordial state.

But in yoga this too has got to change. There is a higher Law than that of physical Matter and that should be progressively and relentlessly imposed on the physical nature. The mind, for instance, has its physical part. It goes on repeating the same old ideas, thought-movements; its gets into a groove of accustomed habits and throws its shadow on every forward thrust of the mind. It is a part of this yogic discipline to loosen the hold of this mechanical mind and shed the ideas and thought-patterns in which the mind tends to live. The mind must be always ready to accept fresh ideas, leaving the old ones behind.

Similarly the desires of the vital, more correctly of the vital physical, should be held in check and gradually cast away. These desires cling and come up in one way or other. They prolong the reign of primitive nature drawing support from the obstinacy of the physical which is their base.

And then there are the attachments that we form, mostly unconsciously, to physical habits. These enter into almost every segment of our daily life and the least attempted change upsets everything. We are so strongly involved in these attachments to physical needs, physical comforts, physical desires, physical positions, physical responses, that every step to break them raises a host of negative reactions. But it has to be done, if we are to get out of the domination of the physical consciousness.

Sri Aurobindo and the Mother repeatedly speak of the dour opposition of physical consciousness, physical nature, to every attempt to introduce a higher consciousness. They defeat such efforts again and again. But persistence and evocation of still higher charges of Consciousness tells in the long run. For this we have to do our home-work tirelessly and thoroughly.

7

SEEING GOD IN OTHERS

How do you do that? Especially when you are face to face with an embodiment of wickedness, some one who is cruel to the bones, a beast in human form? The facts are too forbidding to permit any divinity in the person. Even as a mental notion, it does not work. And still the time-honoured counsel to the seeker is to regard the Divine in all.

Bear in mind that a person as he appears or functions is not all of himself. Behind the exterior, there is something that sustains him through all his perversities. There is a soul which is not touched by any of the outer deformations. Sri Aurobindo describes how when he had the realisation of Lord Vasudeva, the Universal Divine, in Alipore jail, he literally beheld the Lord in every one around, including the convicts in whose 'misused boides', he saw the unmistakable God.

What is required is a conviction that God dwells in every one. This must be built into a strong faith in the being. Next, one must unlearn the habit of stopping the gaze at appearances. The sight must bore through apparent contradictions to what is at the core. In other words the consciousness must be developed. Whether in the mind or in the heart, the consciousness must be widened and deepened so that it does not get blinded or halted at the surface levels but takes a larger and deeper view of things. It must be cultured to translate its theoretical knowledge into practice.

Further, the psychic must be made more and more active. It must be drawn out and helped to extend its influence in daily life. The psychic is divine by nature and it vibrates to the presence of the Divine everywhere. It looks for the Presence and informs the other members of the being. Even when the instrumental faculties are blinded by happenings and appearances, the psychic sends up its message. The seeker learns to listen to it and probe deeper for the truth of things.

Unregenerate nature deforms the becoming of the evolving soul. It falsifies the impulse of the soul. But this does not extinguish the light within, however small. It may be covered as with smoke but it exists nevertheless. Spiritual sight is fixed on this truth of divinity at the core and is not deflected by misleading signals on the surface.

Naturally the seeker recognises the full extent of the deformation. But on that account he does not condemn outright. He learns to understand the causes of such deviations and has more of pity than censure in his attitude. He looks for some saving feature in the offending party through which he contacts the Divinity deep within. Such a regard has a double effect: it elevates the consciousness of the seeker; it also draws out the best in the other, by and by, and prepares for a change in him.

8

WORK AND SADHANA

It is a common experience with those who turn to spiritual life that they lose interest in work. There is a strong disinclination to 'waste' time and energy in occupations that can only lengthen the chain of karma and keep one away from the one thing to be done. This is explicable. For the usual activity in life is carried on under the drive of desire. The vital goads with the ego as the fulcrum. When this motive of ego-desire is given up—as it has to be in spiritual life—there is lack of incentive. The vital is sullen because it is denied its satisfaction. The tamas in the physical rushes up to fill the gap and there is no further interest in working.

But this can only be a phase at the beginning. For, as stated in the Gita, action is the law of life. One has to act. Even a seeker who has made his choice of spiritual destiny has to work, to expend his energies, on some level or another. The way for him is to accept whatever activity is expected of him but execute it in a different spirit. It goes without saying that he renounces the usual desire-motive. He does the work as an offering of his energies to God. Consequently he does not work for the fruits of that work; he learns to take what comes as the will of God. In the process he lifts himself beyond the operation of the law of karma.

That is because he is not personally involved in the activity. There is no personal motivation, no personal seeking for fruit. Not to be involved means not to be totally identified with the action and lost in it. The sadhaka functions as an instrument of a higher Shakti; he lets his nature exert itself to the best of its capacity, but he keeps his own self detached, above the current. He watches, controls, corrects the movement, but does not forget himself in it.

Further he takes care not to get attached to the work he is called upon to do. It is human nature to develop preference to what it is accustomed to. It clings to routine. There is reluctance in the physical nature to any change. The sadhaka is careful to avoid this trap. He is ready to take on whatever work comes to him, as an assignment from God. He does not permit any personal attachment to develop.

Above all he is attentive to the spirit of consecration that should govern the whole movement. That changes the character of work. When so done, action no more binds; it becomes a means for liberation. It elevates nature, brings a deeper or higher consciousness to bear on the situation. Work becomes sadhana.

9

FORM AND PRESENCE

There are lines of sadhana in which meditation on a Form of God is enjoined. Usually it is a visualisation of the Form of a Deity as described in the *dhyāna-sloka*, invocative verse. Or, in rare cases, it is a Form that reveals itself to the seeker. In either case the Form is not a figure of imagination. As Sri Aurobindo describes it, these Forms of Gods are either self-revealed to the human being as an act of Grace or they are what have taken shape in the consciousness of the worshipper or adoring artist and accepted by the Divine.

The Form is a special embodiment of the Consciousness of the Divine Being for work on the particular plane: on the physical plane it is a physical Form, on subtler planes it will be correspondingly subtle. The one advantage for the seeker in having a Form to focus upon is that it becomes a productive channel of communication with the Divine. It is difficult for all to function in an abstract context. But it also limits. The sadhaka is prone to identify the Divine with that particular Form and no other and thus shut himself from other possible manifestations.

Further, Form is only one mode of the revelation of the Divine. The Divine, says the scripture, is both with form and without form, *murta* and *amurta*. Divine without Form is experienced as a Presence. And this Presence is both personal and impersonal. Usually it is impersonal but it is also experienced as a specific Entity. There is a concrete sense of Something present with a benevolent, warming effect. It carries a definite assurance with it of its advent in the atmosphere. One feels it, at times, accompanying one. Some others may need to invoke the Presence and it is there. This Presence is not anything vague and subjective. It carries some characteristic quality of the Deity to which it belongs and leaves no doubt of its character. Thus the Presence of Mahakali will carry a charge of Force; that of Mahalakshmi exude Felicity, Harmony. The Presence of Lord Krishna may be further augmented by notes of the celestial Flute and so on.

For a sadhaka it is perhaps advisable to seek the Presence rather than Form. For forms can be easily imitated. There have been many cases in which the Adversary has taken the form of the chosen Deity and misled the human. It is more difficult to simulate the Divine's Presence. Even if something claims to be that, its vibration will be different, its flavour different. There is likely to be something eerie about it, something cold and foreign.

For one who is sensitive, pure enough in his aspiration, the Presence is unmistakable. He learns to identify himself with it, lose himself in its folds; he refers everything to the Presence—which unveils its personal truth in time—and lets himself be lived by it. What begins as a shadow develops into a palpable Entity whose impact is not confined to the sadhaka alone.

10

YOGA AND MADNESS

Indian spiritual tradition recognises, among the types of liberated beings, the *pisācavat*, demonic, the *unmattavat*, intoxicated. These, though in union with the Divine Consciousness, act unpredictably: crudely, rudely, violently, abominably. We do not speak of them at the moment. We have in mind those who suddenly go berserk in the course of their yoga. They get mentally deranged and make a sad spectacle. And such cases are not rare, they are pretty common, leading the uninformed to blame yoga for causing madness.

Actually the right practice of yoga never causes imbalance. It can only promote better health of mind and soul. It increases self-control, capacities of nature and refines the consciousness. At times when one makes a decided advance and there is some radical change in consciousness within, the outer being fails to keep pace. That may be due to either neglect of the necessity of culturing the instrumental nature alongside inner development or incapacity of certain parts of nature to change. The result is a pronounced disequilibrium between the inner consciousness and the external nature, leading to disorder, unregulated action in life.

It is also possible that some erotic tendency or ambition that were originally concealed, come up and seize the situation created by the yogic development of powers and new openings. They replace the spiritual motivation and the practitioners become either maniacs or titanic egotists. Such persons with a latent deviation at the very start open to various forces in the vital region in the course of their practices and become instruments of those hostile elements. They go off the track and lose their balance.

Thus it is not practice of yoga that leads to these unfortunate developments, but want of sincerity in the person. This insincerity clouds the vision, cuts off discrimination and in all ways pushes the practicer on a suicidal—spiritually disastrous—course. With some this deviation is conscious and they become exploiters of the credulous. But there are others who are not aware of their subconscious impulses or they are too weak to resist them; they lose their reason and are mentally disturbed. It is possible to reclaim such persons with understanding, sympathetic handling and exposing them to corrective influences emanating from saints and other benevolent spiritual personalities. There are also ways of invoking the aid of higher Deities for the purpose. It is possible to succeed with those who are weak but next to impossible with those who are insincere.

There have been cases of mental derangement—at any rate appearing to be so—in our Ashram. Usually the Mother would treat them as cases of some disharmony between the inner and the outer being, help them inwardly to bridge the gulf and ask the community to treat them as if normal. This worked in many cases and the persons returned to normalcy in time.

11

EXPERIENCES

It is rightly said that conclusions of the reasoning mind cannot be always definitive. With different premises, different conclusions are inevitable. This is particularly so in the spiritual province. Here it is experience that is authentic, not reason. True, experiences too cannot be exclusive. After all the Reality or the Consciousness that is experienced has many aspects, many grades of manifestation. We need to take this fact into account while asserting the supremacy of any single experience.

Each experience is true in so far as it answers to some facet of the Reality. Another person may have a totally different experience. The two experiences may appear to be contradictory to each other. The same person too may have such experiences—contradicting each other—over a stretch of time. In such cases, the experiences must not be interfered with; there need be no hurry to explain and interpret them. Apart from the fact that expression limits an experience, deforms it to a certain extent because of the limitations of the human language, the mental and psychological background of the person influences the way he looks at it and draws its meaning.

In yoga these experiences must be allowed to take place without any kind of meddling. The sadhaka watches, notes and makes it part of his knowledge. He does not question the authenticity of another experience simply because it is of a different line. He allows experiences to add up till he gets one which reconciles all that have gone before.

We see a capital illustration of this feature in Sri Aurobindo's early years in yoga. He took to yoga with a positive approach affirming the reality of the world as a manifestation of God. He sought from yoga help to realise the Divine Truth of Knowledge and Power in life in order to elevate and transform the nature of life. But the major realisation that he had under the guidance of Yogi Lele was one of Nirvana. The world appeared to him as a passing show with fleeting images and only the Self real. Sri Aurobindo did not, however, rush to conclusions and convict the world of unreality. He allowed the realisation to settle and organise itself and himself waited without any anticipation or expectation. Gradually he began to get experiences which affirmed the Presence of the Divine in stone Images; ways were opened to him to commune with the Divine Lord presiding over and guiding the universe. He had an unmistakable realisation of the universal Godhead, Lord Vasudeva. In between he did have experiences of the vacant Infinite while in the mountains. He received them all in his expansive consciousness without taking any of them as the ultimate truth. Later he had the vaster realisation revealing to him the transcendent status of the Reality of which the Personal and the Impersonal, Being and Becoming, Qualities and No-qualities, are concurrent aspects. The Supreme is all these and more than these. In itself it is ineffable.

Thus while each experience has a truth of its own, its own relevance, none can be exclusively true. One does not cancel the other. Each has its place in the total scheme. It depends upon where one is at the moment. It is unwise to rush to judgment on the strength of a single experience, however powerful.

12

LIMITATIONS OF REASON

"Reason was the helper, reason is the bar", observes Sri Aurobindo in mentioning its role in the evolution of man. Reason discriminates, sifts the right from the wrong, organises the information so obtained, coordinates various movements of nature. In so many ways it plays an important part in life. It has its domain of activity, its parameters for functioning. A characteristic mode of its operation is to cut up what is whole and analyse the part in itself and come to conclusions. Its look is clipped and working segmented. This serves a purpose at a certain stage in the development of the human mind. But when this faculty of reason seeks to extend its operation to areas that are clearly beyond its range, there arises the possibility of error.

Truth, as we now know, is infinite. It has many sides and each one of them has its own truth which makes it exist. It may be a deformed truth or a partial truth, all the same the element of truth is there in each. For reason, however, what it sees as the truth is the sole truth. It does not recognise that there can be other truths or aspects of the total truth. To realise this fact human reason has to widen itself, elevate itself into a higher reason. As Sri Aurobindo would put it, reason has to be reasonable. Reasonable enough to recognise that it is not infallible. Changing conditions may force it to revise its conclusions. Behind every reasoning there hangs the shadow of doubt. Reason is constantly faced with contradictions which, however, are held as true by other minds. It takes time for reason to learn that no standpoint is absolutely right. It matures, if it is healthy, into realising the justification of opposing positions. It sees that there can be no finality about its conclusions and it begins to doubt itself:

An inconclusive play is Reason's toil.
Each strong idea can use her as its tool;
Accepting every brief she pleads her case.
Open to every thought, she cannot know.

—*Sri Aurobindo*

For true knowledge reason has to exceed itself, acquire a more comprehensive vision and learn to suspend its judgment until it has surveyed all sides of a situation. In other words it must grow into higher reason which reconcilies the apparently contradictory positions or experiences in the context of the total truth of things. Then does one realise that contraries at one level of existence turn to be complementaries at a higher level and that both the roles are part of a larger process of evolving Nature.

13

MORE OF THE PSYCHIC

When the psychic awakes there is powerful current of devotion, *bhakti*, in the heart region. There is a spontaneous flow of feelings of self-giving, adoration. Tears rush to the eyes for no apparent reason. But these tears are tears of joy, tears that purify. The devotee feels a child of the Divine. At times this extends to every one around: he feels a child of everybody.

There is, however, a distinction between these movements issuing from the psychic and somewhat similar emotions that surge up in the heart and a little below. There are strong gusts of devotional expressions. There are dramatic outbursts of weeping for the Divine. There arise imaginative expectations of response from the Divine and if there be delay in it, or if the response does not come forth, or does not come in the way that is wanted there is a kind of revolt—romantically described as *abhimān*, wounded self-respect, and there follows a bout of bitter complaint, plaintive suffering. All these are vital movements which sweep away the seeker from the right course. Unlike the psychic manifestations which are not showy, have no element of claim but are gentle with the dignity of the soul, these vital manifestations are crude and too humanised.

Bhakti is not the whole of the psychic movement. It is only one aspect. The psychic casts its influence on the mind too. When this takes place there is a loosening of the rigidities in the attitudes and workings of the mind. There is more of sympathetic understanding, supportive identification in daily life. Even in the realm of thought, there is a readiness to admit alternate positions. Dogma, narrowness, combative argument, fall off and the mental being gets free from the clamps of the vital and the physical parts. The psychic discrimination between the right and the wrong, truth and error, acts spontaneously when the mind comes fully under the light of the psychic. After all the psychic is directly derived from the Divine Being and it imparts its nature to every part that is open to it, more so the mind which is normally the most evolved part of man.

That is why intellectuals do not need to shy away from the psychic saying that it is an affair of the heart. The intellect too undergoes a modification which, if encouraged, develops into a gradual spiritualisation of the mind. Finally, the psychic plays an important part in the eventual transformation of the human mind into the divine mind.

14

IDEA *vs.* FAITH

Belief is not faith. Neither is idea or conclusion. They are mental in their origin and operation. An idea may possess the mind and shape its activities but that is not faith. Even if the idea is possessed of some evident power, its character is still mental.

Faith, on the other hand, has deeper origins. Usually it is a reflection in the mind of some glimpse of truth deep down in the being. It is anterior to the mind. When this glimpse of truth is not a passing perception but a settled fact that has captured the soul, it communicates itself to the other members of the being as a firm anchor. An aspiration to actualise it in life grows and invades the rest of oneself. In the mind it reflects itself as a strong conviction which cannot be challenged by reasoning or logic. It is possible that the faith may lend itself to be rationally justified, but its existence does not depend upon the sanction of the rationalising intelligence. We will turn to this aspect later.

This faith has power. It gives strength to the being. The mind has a firm basis for its functioning, a direction which is unmistakable. The emotions are inspired by this central faith. The vital too is influenced by this faith and draws its strength from it. It is less easy for the body to share in this faith. Its allegiance is to different age-old laws and its very materiality resists the action of faith on it. Still, it is possible to impose faith on the body gradually and once this is done, the body is the most solid base for the faith to function in life.

Faith may be questioned, challenged by happenings in life. But it has a way of surviving all trials; even if forsaken for a while by the surface being, it returns in some moment of crisis and asserts itself.

Does faith have to stand the test of reason? Not at all, says a high authority, on the other hand the only true faith is what is not based upon reason. While we would not go so far as to take it literally, we recognise that faith does not depend upon reasoning. It may fortify itself with enlightened reason but its source is deeper. The Gita has it that faith provides the root, man is what his faith is.

15

INTUITION IN LIFE

Intuition is an edge or ray of truth. It is an unlaboured presentation of what is sought for: a direction, a solution, a pointer. It is a communication from true Knowledge and is often lost in the mass of thoughts and feelings that run over man all the time. It is a special faculty which is active under various guises. What we call instinct is really a veiled form of intuition, especially the instinct that is common where the mind is not very active with its reason, doubt and lack of certainty.

We see it in the animal kingdom. They function with a sure instinct. Also at the human stage in evolution, the primitive man whose intellect is yet to be developed runs his life largely on his instinctive impulses. That is the way Nature leads him. Even in the present stage of human evolution, the man of action is guided more by insight which is a half-intuition or a vital intuition than by his reason. The mental man, who lives mostly as led by thought, intellect, reasoning, is not normally open to the action of intuition. Each time it comes in the form of a flash or a sudden suggestion, the doubting mind steps in, questions it, doubts its correctness. Even if it is received in the being there is some mixture; other faculties of the mind rush up and dilute or discolour the original intuitive feeling or thought.

It is the intention of Nature that what functions as veiled intuition in the form of instinct at the sub-mental levels should be recovered in its unveiled and direct action at the higher mental stage of evolution. A special discipline of consciousness is necessary for this purpose.

In the first place one must learn to quieten the mind. It is only when the mind is reasonably quiet, free from restless activity of thoughts, that faculties like intuition get a chance to make themselves felt. And when it acts—in the form of a suggestion or an unmistakable feeling—it must be allowed to settle without interference. The discriminating sense should step in only after the visitor has taken his seat.

Sri Aurobindo counsels against confining the action of intuition to a specialised field only, say poetry, mathematics etc. It should be encouraged to play a part in one's general life too. That builds up a habit, a climate in which intuition can organise itself as a working faculty. And this is not limited to the mind. We know there is a vital intuition which is less prone to inteference by the mental operations like doubt. The vital intuition has a drive of its own and it pushes aside all hesitations from the cautious mind. Similarly there is an intuition in the body which is almost infallible. One must cultivate it, pay attention to the promptings of the body; even in what may be considered to be 'small', 'insignificant' details the body-intuition is alert.

16

VISHWA MANAVA

Man is normally limited to his own interests; next he is involved in his family—his extended interests. It is only in an indirect manner that he owns—or is obliged to own—his responsibilities as a member of the society in which he lives. In other words he is centred round his ego-self. He lives in a personal world of his own;

his thoughts, feelings, impulses, activities, all are organised around the well-being of himself and those who serve him.

This, however, is only a stage in his evolution. Sooner or later he is pressured, by circumstances from without or promptings from within, to expand the range of his concerns. As he grows in consciousness, in knowledge, he realises that his true welfare is bound up with the welfare of the collectivity of which he is a part. He identifies himself with the needs and aspirations of the society. It is thus that evolutionary Nature leads the individual man through progressively widening rounds till he arrives at the stage where he identifies himself with the entire humanity. He becomes a humanist, in the widest sense, and is on his way to become the universal man.

Poets have sung the glories of this unique person whose mind, life and even physical movements are in tune with the rhythms of universal Nature, who embodies in himself the aspirations, hopes and vision of mankind. His is the religion of humanity. But this is more an ideal that may be approximated to but hardly ever actualised. Mere mental refinement, conviction, enlargement of vision, service for the good of the race, cannot produce the universal consciousness in which alone there are no barriers between the individual and the universal manifestations. Sri Aurobindo describes in unforgettable lines:

> He felt the beating life in other men
> Invade him with their happiness and their grief;
> Their love, their anger, their unspoken hopes
> Entered in currents or in pouring waves
> Into the immobile ocean of his calm.

He heard the inspired sound of his own thoughts
Re-echoed in the vault of other minds;
The world's thought-streams travelled into his
ken;
His inner self grew near to others' selves
—(*Savitri* 1.3)

Naturally this radical change cannot be effected only by mental effort. Only a deeper, spiritual, culturing can bring about this widening. A personal discovery of the inner Self—not that which turns away from the world towards a transcendence, but the Self that is one with the Self of All—and living in the consciousness of the Self, is indispensable for this development.

It may be noted that even in the case of such a universal person the shadow of Ignorance still falls on his nature. He is still subject to error. All the possibilities in human nature are still awake in him, whether they be high or low. Man has to go beyond the reign of the Overmind and step into the Zone of Truth for a truly divine life of truth and unity to become possible.

17

ART AND FORM

There are some who hold that in a work of art it is the Idea, the Vision of the artist, that is important. Equally important, assert others, is the form given to the conception. Actually it is both that are relevant in the context. Sri Aurobindo points out that if the vision is the soul, form is the body of art. Both the soul and body go together.

Form is not just a visual support. In manifestation, form is a must. The formless takes form and brings out the hidden realities. And this figure corresponds to the nature of the contents that ensoul it. The lines and designs are not assembled somehow by Nature, the great artist of life or by the human artist. There is a meaning in each line, each contour. Each gives a clue to the quality of the substance within.

There are several ingredients in the making of form. The dimensions, the subtle nuances of hues, their mutual congruence and the right coordination among all the constituents of the design—all come into the picture. When these are perfect we have beauty. The beauty of a work of art does not decay with time. It throbs with life and adds a freshness moment to moment.

We may add that this form (in art) is not anything artificial. Like the words of a poet which form themselves without effort under the impulsion of his soul, the makings of form shape themselves without a self-conscious design on the part of the artist. The vision, the idea, casts itself into its appropriate body. He lets it form naturally. The Inspiration finds its way to delineate itself in the way it chooses.

18

POETS AND INTELLIGIBILITY

We are speaking of poets who are moved to express themselves by some experience, especially of the spiritual or mystic kind. Do they have to make an effort to make themselves understood by the common reader? No, says Sri Aurobindo. The poet is concerned solely with articulating his inner experience. He needs to keep himself as passive as possible so that the message gets through with the least interference, in as accurate a rendering as possible.

We do not ask such questions when we stand face to face with a Seer like Dirghatamas, the celebrated blind Rishi of the Veda. We may not understand what he says at the first reading. But we are overwhelmed. We are in the presence of some profound experience which has power to impact on our being even today, thousands of years after the hymn saw the light of the day. If we do not get the meaning, we do not blame the poet; we try to tune ourselves with the mind of the seer and let the idea sink into us, first through the medium of sound and then through the thought formation. It is evident that the hymnodist is concerned with 'carving out' the hymn from the recesses of his inner being as faithfully as possible to his mighty experience.

Of course this does not mean that the poet is totally indifferent to the form of his creation or to the structure of his utterance. He does take care to acquaint himself with the science of prosody, metre, sound effect. That is why Chhandas, metrical knowledge, was a part of the education imparted to the student of the Vedic Knowledge in olden days. The better one is equipped in this regard, the more likely is the inspiration to flow into these prepared channels without.

19

IDENTIFICATION WITH CHARACTERS

A successful writer of plays like Shakespeare, a poet-creator of an epic like Vyasa do not make a distinction between major characters and minor ones as far as their attention is concerned. Every character is treated individually and made alive. The poet identifies himself with the characters, makes each a part of his creative becoming. His interest or preference may lie in any one or two, but all are filled with the consciousness of the creator.

Valmiki does not spare himself while delineating the personality of Ravana on the ground that his real interest is in glorifying the avatarhood of Sri Rama. Whether the character is a friend of the Ideal sought to be upheld or he is a foe, the poet gives his best in presenting him. Speaking of Ravana, the titan-king, we almost come to admire his one-pointed dedication to austerities to win the Grace of God Shiva. He has his own code of behaviour which is worthy of emulation in many respects. Valmiki's genius lives as every one of his creations. That is why his epic is lauded as preeminent in the hoary tradition of India.

Similarly in his epic *Savitri*, Sri Aurobindo is lavish in his characterisation of the God of Death. The majesty, the calm hauteur of his figure almost makes us forget that he is the destroyer from whose net none can escape. Even when he speaks slightingly of the values we cherish, of God the benevolent creator and protector of all, he compels a smile of indulgence at his sophistry. The reader never comes to hate this dark Godhead. Behind all stands the assurance of the poet that the dark gods, no less than the white ones, are also the children of the same Mother of Love.

In all great creations of this kind, the poet identifies himself with the character inly. That is why he is able to give us a peep into the workings of the mind of the antagonist, even, at times, to the point of justification.

Of course we are left in no doubt where the sympathies of the poet lie but of his fairness to the contras there is no question.

20

GRACE *vs* EFFORT

It is of course a childish notion that if one surrenders oneself to the Grace, there is no more any necessity of effort. It is another kind of escapism. In the first place to be surrendered fully to the Grace is itself not an easy task. One may make the *sankalpa*, resolve, to surrender but to work it out in all the parts of the being is a sadhana by itself. Usually the decision is in the mind. The emotional being may or may not share in it. The vital may and usually it does, protest and refuse cooperation. The physical with its obstinate attachment to habits takes time to fall in line. It is a day-to-day, even a moment-to-moment programme to live in the spirit of this surrender.

This effort to surrender itself, it must be noted, is originated, sustained and kept growing by an act of Grace. To tune one's will to the Divine Will is the secret of surrender. This implies constant vigilance, self-correction and continuous orientation in one's daily life. One has to be alert to prevent inertia, tamas, from gaining ground under the plea of surrender. Whatever activity needs to be done, has to be done, but in an enabling spirit. One learns to function as an instrument of the higher Will.

Work one must, but without the egoism of the doer. The most that is possible must be put in. But the result is not of one's own labours. The result is an effect of the Grace. This spirit of regarding the result as the act of Grace is important. The test of surrender is here: there should be a readiness to accept any result as coming from the Divine. As it has been graphically put, if the Divine gives what you wish, it is Grace; if the Divine does not, it is double Grace.

21

BINDERS

It is a fact of common experience that whenever one takes up a course of action for some radical change or progress, especially in spiritual life, some difficulty or other comes up very soon. Everything is smooth as long as one keeps to the set grooves of nature and is content to conform. But the moment one seeks to exceed nature, steps beyond the accustomed boundaries, obstacles are thrown up. Many give up when confronted with these oppositions in life. Some feel it is not worth the trouble of grappling with the new situations; some others take it that things are not meant to be that way and draw back to their habitual rounds.

Actually these obstacles are not meant to discourage effort. They are intended, on the other hand, to stimulate and prod for greater efforts to break a new line. In sadhana, particularly, the obstacles show the deficiencies in one's nature which are to be made up before further progress is possible. It is in this sense that the hostile forces are looked upon as necessary agents to spotlight the lacunae in the sadhaka and force him to make good before proceeding further. The difficulties are there with design. Taken in the right spirit they turn out to be helpful factors in ensuring stable bases for the aspired growth.

Each obstacle has a message. One needs to pause and look into oneself to find out what could have caused the complication. Though the causes may appear to be external, an honest scrutiny usually reveals some lack in oneself which has invited the particular development. The right inner adjustment does bring about a change in the outer circumstances. Even otherwise the effort steels the strength of the seeker. And that is the purpose of the challenge.

The Rishis of the Veda speak of such obstacles in the spiritual path as binders, *nidah.* They hold you down and do not allow you to proceed until you have faced the problem squarely and solved it effectively. It is only when you have covered the territory and are equipped to go further, that they give the 'password' to advance. They concede to you the right to go beyond their own reign. Thus does the Rishi pray:

> May the Binders tell us, 'Forth now and push forward also in other fields and conquer them.'
>
> —(*Rig Veda,* 1.4.5)

26-7-'87

22

DAWNS

When the Vedic Rishi speaks of the Dawn, he does not refer to the daily dawn in our physical world. The Dawn he prays to is a spiritual dawn. In the course of his tapasya scaling the heights of his being, opening new dimensions of his consciousness, he comes across many a subtle phenomenon. He hears different kinds of sounds, he sees several types of symbols. They are all fingerprints of the leading Consciousness. It is a capital event to the seeker when there is an entry of light on the inner horizon. It may be in the form of bright rays of light or an emergence of a glow of light. That is the first sign of a break-through round the corner. Normally, however, it fades away leaving a happy memory, a feeling of a threshold. The Rishi prays fervently to the Dawn to appear again. Some of the most beautiful hymns in the Veda are these evocatory prayers to Ushas, the Goddess of Dawn. They laud her glory, describe how the Night breaks with the arrival of the Dawn, they look forward with intense longing to her advent. Thus there are repeated breaks of Dawn, accustoming the being of the Rishi to the impact of the higher Radiances.

Sings the Seer Kutsa Angirasa:

> She follows to the goal of those that are passing on beyond, she is the first in the eternal succession of the dawns that are coming.

To a question, how can there be a *first* dawn if there be an eternal succession of dawns, Sri Aurobindo answers revealingly. He points out that it is the first for those who are to come, the last for those who are passing.

When the initial emergence of light takes place in the being of the Rishi, that is the first Dawn. It may recede but it is followed by another when conditions are ready for it. This one too is succeeded by still another. And so on. After a series of these outbreaks and recedings, the Dawn spreads out into the Day: the spiritual Light steadily grows and spreads its illumination. The Rishi has witnessed the last Dawn in the series that

have passed. He walks in the full light of the Day with the Sun of Truth ascending to the meridian.
27-7-'87

23

CONCERNING MEDITATION

And still the questions pour in. So much has been written on the theory and practice of meditation. So many brands of meditation have been popularly presented for instant results. But they do not seem to have helped the avid prospective enthusiasts very much. Almost every day some one or other comes asking how to meditate. And there are quite a number who ask an omnibus question, what is meditation. The other day an intelligent visitor mentioned that a friend of his had devoted years to the practice of meditation and yet he had arrived nowhere. Is there any help to such frustrated persons?

The difficulty in answering these queries is that most have preconceived ideas of what meditation is, or should be. They think in terms of 'courses'; some even ask for crash courses. It takes them time to understand that there is not one process of meditation but a hundred. Each type is in keeping with its objective. The type of meditation meant for you depends upon the purpose for which you want it. But of course there are certain features common to all.

To begin with, to simply sit with closed eyes is no meditation. You sit in this position and allow things to happen. Thoughts run about, may be with added rush because there is no other occupation for the mind. You may sit for hours together but nothing is likely to ensue.

You must have an objective. The mind must be centred around this objective e.g. Peace, Silence, God Shiva or Krishna, your Guru or any theme dear to your heart. It is easy to start with this focus. But very soon distracting thought-movements are likely to interfere and you go off at a tangent. You need to come back to your centre. This means practice. You must make it a practice to sit for meditation at regular hours. Instead of sitting for hours at a time, it is advisable to sit for brief periods more times a day. That helps the system to acclimatise itself to the practice. Sri Aurobindo observes that more hours of meditation does not necessarily mean more progress. What is important is what happens during these sessions of meditation? Is it what Mother calls, stagnant meditation or a dynamic one?

Stagnant meditation is that in which you let things take place. Whatever is uppermost in your nature at that time gets an upperhand and carries you with it. You are passive. If you mean business, the meditation must be an active one. You have to be vigilant to reject irrelevant movements and promote those that feed your aspiration. Now the object of serious meditation is to get away from the hurly-burly of common life and get into a state of consciousness which takes you out of the pulls of nature—at any rate for the time being—and makes you restful and open to a settling of peace or calm in the being. You learn to tune yourself with a higher or a deeper consciousness. Each sitting helps you to forge this link again and again till it becomes natural.

In the beginning you may get sleep. This is common. For when the body is not in movement and the senses are withdrawn from their outer objects, the first reaction is of lapse into inertia, sleep. But that is only temporary. Even while the state of sleep occupies the surface being, some activity goes on within. This sleep is not the same as the sleep when you are in bed.

In this connection the posture becomes important. It is advised that one must sit erect: the chest, the neck and the head must be in a straight line. This ensures that the spine is erect and consequently there is a free flow of energies in the body. If the posture is bent or slanting there is an evident obstruction. It goes without saying that a horizontal position is unsuited as it invites sleep.

It may happen, in some cases, that as one goes deeper, the body undergoes many involuntary postures. It may start shaking or rocking. This indicates some lack of balance in the system: the body is unable to bear and sustain the inflow of energies and tries to adjust itself by such movements. While these movements —some of them quite ungainly—are lauded as signs of yogic activity in certain lines of Yoga, they are discouraged in the Poorna Yoga. Any movement which is unconscious must be arrested and brought under control. Some of the Hatha Yogic asanas are helpful to establish stability in the body and promote endurance of inrushes natural in yoga.

We spoke of active meditation, meaning thereby a practice which ensures the right movement of consciousness. The aspiration must be kept alive. In the earlier stages one needs to ignite the flame again and again. The one problem that faces the aspirant is of invasion of thoughts. Of the several ways that are open to the practitioner, the best one is not to fight with the thoughts. One should ignore them, keeping the attention centred on the purpose of meditation. The thoughts are allowed to play on the peripheries of the mind. In the absence of participation by the mind, they weaken and pose no further problem.

Some tend to get into states of semi-unconsciousness. But one must take care not to get stuck in them. Even before one begins the session, one must put a strong will against being dragged into unconsciousness and build up an aspiration to grow into a higher or deeper consciousness. Again and again one needs to remind oneself of this necessity of crossing the threshold.

It is quite disconcerting to find oneself ultra-sensitive to external impacts during these exercises of meditation. One may be in a fine state of peace during meditation but on coming out of it, the slightest disturbance brings out a disproportionate reaction of anger, upset. It may be for a brief moment but the havoc is done. This is due to lack of harmony between the part that participates in the meditation and the vital which is normally left out. It resents being starved and sets up a turmoil at the first opportunity. Thus it is that one is advised to be extra-careful after meditation so as not to play into the hands of the negative elements. We may remark in passing that this caution is necessary when any kind of spiritual advance is made. Forces in nature are on the wait to pull you down the moment you feel satisfied that you have progressed and achieved.

28-7-'87

(ii)

Naturally one first needs to gather oneself. One is normally so spread out in thoughts, feelings, impulsions that it requires some effort to draw back all of oneself. And where does one gather oneself thus? There are two locations—or three—that are enjoined. The centre of indrawal may be the heart region. Or it could be the centre between the eye-brows. Or above the head or behind it. One gradually narrows the area of awareness and gathers in any of these centres. How to decide which centre is to be chosen? Usually one's nature indicates where it is easier to do so. One moves naturally towards the centre where nature has prepared oneself. It is not easy to withdraw from all preoccupations this way. To reverse the trend of nature is a task that calls for will-power. A little of deep breathing is helpful at this stage to slow down the multiple movements of nature and control the mind. We do not speak here of Pranayama. That is a science by itself and has its use for other purposes. Slow down the breathing, observe the breath, you will find yourself becoming quiet. It is easier then to settle yourself in the chosen centre.

The faculties thus gathered need a focus to stay. Here comes the stage of concentration which is so often confused with meditation. In concentration you fix your attention on something. It may be an image, a flame or a likeness of the Deity (as prescribed) or of the Guru; it may be a sound, a mantra given by the Guru; or it may be an Idea viz. God as Love, as Beauty, as Peace, as Shakti and so on. You stay fixed to it. Even if you are distracted by thoughts, each time you become aware of it you come back to your theme. It is understood that this kind of concentration cannot be a prolonged operation. You let your consciousness flow on your chosen theme. It dwells upon it, works it out in several ways. This dwelling of consciousness in a single-pointed movement on an object is meditation, dhyana. Your mind flows, it is said, like oil in the wick—steadily and continuously.

It may happen at times that in the course of this exercise, when you are thus lost in the movement of meditation, everything in your body slows down. The blood-circulation, the heart-beat, the pulse, become slower and slower to the point where you fear a total stoppage. A fear arises that death may take place. It is an unnerving experience which many have had and some have rushed out of the experience in panic. But it is only a nervous reaction. Even if the physical breathing were to slow down to the point of cessation, there is a subtle breathing which keeps you alive. The fear is baseless. Sri Aurobindo points out that it is the fear of the ego at the prospect of being swallowed up by the Infinite. Keep this in mind and you will be able to smile if such fear arises in you during meditation.

During the course of the sitting, you may have visions. They may relate to possible happenings or visual precipitations of your own secret hopes or fears; they may be figures or colours, most of them symbolic. While there are traditional meanings attached to these symbol-shapes, the precise significance has something to do with the turn of your nature and background also. Do not be in hurry to interpret these visions. Most of them occur on the vital plane; they are not necessarily spiritual. Similarly you may hear various kinds of sounds. Yoga-sastra speaks of ten types of sounds: notes of the flute, cymbals, cricket tones, roar of the sea etc. Do not overvalue them either. Usually both these visions and sounds are indications that your subtle senses have opened and are active on the subtle planes of your being. Note them with a detached spirit. If the sounds pursue you even in other hours when you are occupied otherwise—ignore them. Things settle down after a while.

Read carefully what Sri Aurobindo has said on what he calls the Intermediate Zone where glittering experiences offer themselves and arrest your attention.

Usually they aim at your ego and seek to divert your course. Of course not all have to pass through this Zone. Not all have the visions and sound-experiences we have just spoken about. But on that account do not imagine that you are not progressing in sadhana. It is the growth of consciousness that matters and not your having or not having these experiences.

The growth of spiritual consciousness makes itself felt in unmistakable terms. You are no longer restless; there is more of calm and quietude in your being. You are not easily upset over happenings, there is a growing detachment, an equality. You develop an unfailing trust in the Divine Grace, you have no fear. You can test for yourself your gains or lack of them in your reactions and responses to events in daily life.
29-7-'87

24

JAPA

When Patanjali says *japah tad artha bhāvanam*, that is Japa where the meaning is dwelt upon, it is convincing. In the process of continuous mentation on the significance and the special import of the Name or Mantra, the being of the sadhaka opens itself to the vibrations of the Deity and is bathed in them. The impact is not merely of the sound, physical or subtle; there is a settlement of the ensouling truth of the Mantra in his consciousness. Sooner or later, the results are bound to ensue.

What if one repeats the Mantra without knowing its meaning, or at any rate not being aware of it at the time of the practice? No, say the high-browed, it is a mechanical japa and it comes to nothing. The practitioner may derive some satisfaction by doing so but in truth it can have no effect. But there are so many legends, even factual cases, in which people are reported to have achieved results. When Sri Aurobindo was asked whether there could be any truth in these claims, he answered that even mechanical japa can yield fruit if the psychic is touched by it in some way or the other.

That throws a fresh light on the matter. One may not know the meaning of the Mantra and yet repeat it with deep feeling, with real devotion in the heart. Such an outpouring sends currents of call deep down and there is response from the psychic being which is divine at its core. What is required is sincerity and devotion. The japa must arise on a crest of devotion.

We do not speak here of a Mantra that is communicated by the Guru and vibrates with his power in the being of the disciple. It works on its own regardless of whether the person is aware of the import or not. Each time he repeats the Mantra, there is an automatic link with the dynamis of the Teacher which works unfailingly.

25

SURRENDER: AN ANALYSIS

Surrender begins with a resolve to give oneself to the Divine. This *sankalpa* is usually taken by the mind. If this resolve is of a casual nature it weakens in the course of time and peters away. But if the sadhaka decides upon it seriously, then it spreads out into a firm attitude. In every movement he witholds his personal will and lets himself be guided by what he feels to be the higher will. Gradually this mental attitude is imposed upon the other members of his being. This process of getting the emotional and the vital parts of himself to share in the central attitude of surrender to the Divine is more difficult than cultivating a general attitude. It calls for exertion of the will.

Surrender is generally looked upon as a passive poise. It may be so in the initial stages. But if one is sincere, it has to become an active operation: the *bhāva* has to turn into *kriyā*. Here is the key to the yoga of surrender. The decision of the being that is reflected in the mind as a resolve, must be worked out in each part of oneself in detail. Long-standing habits, grooves of nature, present a formidable opposition. Things are all right as long as one is conscious and vigilant in affirming this movement of submission to the Divine Will. But the moment there is a slight lack of attention, the old Adam returns and has his way. It is no use getting upset or depressed about such lapses. One has to correct the atavistic impulse and take to the track.

This labour of diligent application of the resolve has to continue till the whole nature falls in line and accepts surrender as the law of its life. When this becomes natural, there is no sense of loss or deprivation that may be felt in the earlier stages. There is a positive joy in attuning oneself to the Divine and functioning as his instrument or channel.

6-8-'87.

26

IMPERFECT OFFERING AND THE DIVINE

Any offering to the Divine is tainted by the imperfections of the person who does it. There may be an undercurrent of desire for reward or an appeal for redress. So too with prayers. They are hardly pure in the sense of being absolutely selfless. Traditional spirituality frowns upon such loaded offerings from the humans to the Divine. But as things are men are all imperfect, in one way or the other. Should every one have to wait till he becomes spotlessly pure before he is eligible to approach the Divine?

The Gita is clear on this point. The Lord does not withhold himself from his devotee because of his imperfections. He assures that as men approach him, he receives them. He receives the human in the manner of his approach. He does not wait for every one to become a Jnanin before he is accessible to the supplicant. Again the benevolent Lord declares that there are four classes of devotees: those who seek fulfilment of their needs; those who are in distress; those who seek to know the Divine; those who love him because they know him and realise that he is the sole object of the soul's love. And, we are assured, that all of these are dear to him.

That there is some self-interest in the act of prayer or offering does not disqualify. Every one functions at his level. It is through his present nature that man grows into his higher nature. Thus when he acts naturally he does evoke a response from the Divine. It is of course understood that he has the requisite faith and trust in the compassion of the Divine. What would seem to decide from his end—the lower end—is the quality of his earnestness and dependence upon the Divine.

It is inevitable that commonly some self-motive accompanies the offering in the beginning. But as the desires get more or less fulfilled, the faith deepens, the communion changes its character and the all-too-human elements fall away. One learns to love the Divine for its own sake. One feels it below one's dignity to pray for mundane purposes. The offering becomes an offering of the soul, unadulterated, pure.

One starts from where he is. The Divine too grades the response accordingly. It is through the *aparā*, lower, that we enter into the *parā*, higher. Acceptance of the lower with a view to raising it into the higher is the way; not a total rejection of it, for the higher is present in some way in the lower impelling it from within to move further on.
8-8-'87

27

ON WRITING

The other day some one wrote that he did not believe in writing regularly. He would take up the pen only when he had the 'inspiration'. He was pretty strong against the habit of writing every day whether one was moved to do it or not. Maybe that is his temperament. But there is another side to it.

One is advised to keep on writing regularly. The writing is not done specifically to be put in print but to keep the brain cells that are concerned with this activity in good fettle. In the ancient system of learning they speak of *āvritti*, repetition. It creates grooves in the being—not just in the mind—and the consciousness flows in them whether one is attentive to it or not. Similarly if the habit of writing is made a regular feature, the mind turns to it without effort, with the result that when the inspiration or provocation comes, there is a ready instrument. A rusted apparatus is very discomfiting. So too with singing. Those who want to be good singers, keep a fixed time for the exercise; and they practise whether they are in mood or not, whether the voice is in good condition or not. The vocal chords have got to be kept in working condition always. The same is the case with the cells that attend to writing.

One of our gifted poets was once overcome with disgust for writing. He felt that it would be more profitable to devote that time to pursuits like meditation, prayer and the like. When the matter was referred to Sri Aurobindo he advised against yielding to the 'disgust'. This kind of aversion comes to many at some stage or another. It was pointed out that it is mostly due to *tamas*. It must be rejected.

It could be that at times this is due to fatigue which itself is a result of over-exertion. The fatigue may be in the brain or in the nerves. In such cases the obvious course is to go slow, take a break for a while.

It is like keeping a machine in order. It needs to be run to prevent it from rusting. It is like physical exercise to keep up the health. There may be unavoidable breaks but by and large, regular activation of the limbs is a must for healthy living. The disinclination that creeps on now and then is usually a tamasic pull back.

Note that all writing need not be of the first order. A good deal of pruning and revising is necessary. But

if one goes on writing, after a time things fall in the right pattern. Then it becomes a question of not interfering with the flow. In the zeal for editing the red pencil often scores off the right expressions that have formed at the first touch. Discrimination grows with practice and detachment.
8-8-'87

28

ACTION OF GRACE

True, Grace is unconditional. It does not depend upon one's deserts. The Katha Upanishad is unequivocal on the point. Neither by brain-power nor by learning nor by listening to Wisdom, can one win the Grace. It is only to him whom the Self chooses that it bares its body. Here there is no question of virtue or sin. If reasons it has, the Grace is moved by higher factors, not by man-made standards.

And yet there are conditions to be fulfilled for the action of the Grace. The first is receptivity on the part of the individual. If he is not in a receptive state, the Hour of God goes by. It is possible that the Grace may help to prepare the necessary receptivity. But it is an indirect action. For till the person is so ready, the Grace acts from above, it does not descend in him.

Even if there is a minimum of receptivity, it is enough to begin with. For as the consciousness grows, the receptivity also increases. Mere *tapasyā*, concentrated effort, is not enough to win the objective in spiritual life. The results of the effort do not depend upon the labour. They are gifts of Grace.

Does or can Grace act even without faith on the

part of the recipient? Yes, says Sri Aurobindo. Faith may follow the action of Grace. Grace acts on its own in the scheme of the Divine's manifestation. It is possible, of course, that though the person may not have faith in his external being, it may be there in the soul.

It goes without saying that the Grace acts differently in one who is conscious than in another who is unconscious of it. In the case of the latter the awareness forms as the Grace works.

9-8-'87

29

TAPASYA

It is a wrong notion that tapasya means asceticism. It is neither punishment of the body, denial of the legitimate demands of life. Infliction of physical suffering and pain on oneself in the belief that it takes one nearer God is a pervert superstition. It is an insult to the Indweller, says the Gita.

What, then, is tapasya? It is a concentration of energies for application to achieve a chosen objective. Normally one's faculties are diversely spread out. The energies with which one is endowed are not all active. Those that are active spend themselves in a hundred directions. One may or may not be fully aware of this dissipation. Tapasya means those energies that are pouring out in so many pursuits are drawn back and assembled for a purposive action. Energies that are lying unused, inert, are activised and employed to further the objective.

It is not that tapasya is always hard on oneself, unpleasant to one's nature. If one is sincere in wanting to achieve a particular object, he comes to like the steps he takes, he joys in them and that very satisfaction adds to his intensity. The Upanishads speak of the creative power of *tapas*. Brahman grows by tapas, Brahman creates by tapas. It is the *heat* of incubation that brings out the universe from the Being that is Brahman.

And man follows the example, treads the same Path. Whenever he wants to achieve something, create anything—in any field—he concentrates his energies and pours them to work out his objective. Tapas is the sanctified means of effectuation of one's will.
9-8-'87

30

FORCES AND BEINGS

Force is One. It is the essential Shakti of the Supreme Being. In manifestation this Force deploys itself into many lines of action. It takes on the character of the substance in which it acts. Thus there is a mental force, a vital force, a physical force. And of course there are spiritual forces of various grades, even as there are anti-forces of kinds. These are in fact deformations and deviations from what were originally divine forces.

Let us note that there are no individual forces as such. There are only universal forces. These again have the character of the universal plane on which they function. Speaking of our world, there is a universal Nature with its physical, vital and mental gradations. This Nature puts out forces appropriate to each level of this existence and they act through the individual. He may think and even feel that it is his own force but the fact is otherwise.

Now are these forces entities by themselves, are they beings? They are not. At the head of each group of forces there is a being. These beings have been lauded and worshipped in primitive religions as gods. But they are not. There are beings on the vital and mental planes —benevolent and malevolent—who wield these forces even as there are godheads who direct the forces that are under their command.

Ultimately all forces are emanations of the supreme Shakti which itself belongs to the Supreme Being, the Divine. Shakti implies the Shakta, Power points to the One who holds the Power. At the human level, it is right to treat the forces that operate in life as universal forces which may or may not be admitted by the individual. The individual is endowed with a will that should be exercised to make a selection from the forces that pour into him from Nature. He is not obliged to submit to them as the sub-human creation is. He is in a position to detach himself and rise above Nature. As he rises in the scale of consciousness he learns to operate the higher, occult forces to check and control the activities of the forces of lower Nature.

Speaking of Force and forces, it is helpful to recall Sri Aurobindo's clear-cut distinctions among these agencies of manifestation:

"Force is the essential Shakti; Energy is the working drive of the Force, its active dynamism; Power is the capacity born of the Force; Strength is energy consolidated and stored in the *ādhār*."

10-8-'87

31

SUPRA-TERRESTRIALS

An American mother describes a recurring scene when her son was an infant. She would place him on the dining table and feed him with a spoon. Suddenly the boy would smile and say, 'Hi!' Thinking that somebody must have entered the room evoking the greeting from the little one, she looked back only to find there was none. She got intrigued and asked him who had come. She learnt that some one was there. She had no doubt that it was some angel on seeing whom the boy broke into smiles. Obviously a benevolent one. Herself being a healer of sorts, she was not new to these things.

There are cases of a different genre. Some children are found to be crying for no apparent reason. When asked why, they look with fear in a particular direction and cry still more. Then there was a lady in our Ashram. She would frequently complain that some odd people were peeping at her through her window. Family members were inclined to treat it as a delusion. But the Mother observed that they were real beings from the subtler world. In another connection she cited examples of children seeing such beings and crying; they cannot explain that there are aliens around. They can only cry out their fear. The Mother added that it is a blessing that men cannot see all that goes on around them, with their physical eye. If they did, it would be an awful confusion.

These beings are clearly not imaginary formations. They are real entities from non-physical worlds visiting us for any reason or no reason. Instances are not rare when persons who are on their death-bed cry protestingly that messengers of death have come to take them away. This is not any objectivisation of secret fear. As the life-energy wanes, physical sight gets weaker and their subtler sight becomes active; and they do see these beings ready to escort them. Sri Aurobindo points out that with some, parts of their being are already on the other side and those parts come to face with the denizens of the other world.

It is a fact of recorded experience that those who leave their physical bodies find themselves accosted by a Being or beings of light. As soon as they awake from the swoon that follows the moment of departure, they find it all strange around. They get confused. But very soon they are met by helpful beings who take them across. Tradition has it that holy centres are more propitious for such help to be readily available. The spiritual influence of the saints and yogins who have lived there creates a favourable environment for a smooth transition.

Of course much depends upon the nature of the vibrations one carries. If one is lost in attachments to the earth-life below or one carries the dark shadows of the life that has been none-too-honourable, then the help proffered may be missed or ignored. The Mother spoke of a case or two when certain devotees who had just died did not recognise her as she was standing on the border to help them on. They went on as though blind-folded, lost in their own desire-formations.

Mythology speaks of *yama-dūta*, messengers of Death. These do not meet the humans only after death. At times they do enter into the atmosphere of the person who is dying or due to die and announce themselves. It may be in dream or in a delirium or even in a waking state. The line that separates the physical from the non-physical is very thin.

32

CHANGING OF GURUS

It is a spiritual tradition that once one takes initiation from a Guru, the relation of Guru-disciple stands for the rest of life. There is also a permitted course of *bhramara nyāya*, logic of the bee, in which one goes from Guru to Guru—as from flower to flower—collects honey from each and nourishes himself upon that composite sustenance. What is the right course for an awakened seeker in the face of these contradictory counsels?

Actually as long as a person is in search of the right path for him—for there are several paths to the Destination—he is free to go from person to person, taste something of each teaching. He is not a disciple of anybody; he is still a seeker yet to find his Guide and line of practice. This is particularly applicable to those who are satisfied with the common mode of life; they try and hope to get help and benediction from all possible quarters and it works. But once a person decides upon a serious quest, it is time for him to find out where his affinity lies and choose his Guide. Of course things do not normally happen this way: something in the Guide meant for him draws him like a magnet and the novice gets unmistakable signs of where his destiny lies.

Thereafter the aspirant will do well not to flit from Guru to Guru. Each Guru has his approach, his way, his goal. The influence of one may—and usually does—

conflict with that of others. It is not a question of all roads leading to Rome. The Divine Reality has several aspects and each aspect has its route of realisation. Different Teachers have different goals marked out for them. Influences can thus dilute each other if not contradict. The influence of an Adwaita Teacher, for instance, is bound to create friction with that of a Dualist Teacher. The sadhaka can ill afford to sport such contradictions in himself. He must have good-will for all, respect for all Gurus, but as far as he is concerned he is open only to the Guru that is chosen for him by the Divine.

What is one to do when the Guru leaves his body? Who is to guide? A frequently asked question, nevertheless an academic one. For to a sadhaka on the path, his Guru never dies. He may leave his physical sheath, but he continues, his consciousness continues in a concrete way, to guide him, to lead him. Once the Guru enters the being of the disciple, he stays there for ever. We do not speak of exceptions which are rare.

It may happen that the Guru himself may indicate to his disciples who is to take his place after his passing. In such cases, he makes the necessary occult adjustments to facilitate the transfer. Though rare, such instances are there in spiritual history. We have the famous example of Nagai Japta, Guru of many in South India, asking his disciples to await the arrival of a Poorna Yogi from the north to take his place: Sri Aurobindo.

12-8-'87

33

NERVOUS AURA

The Upanishad speaks of five sheaths, the physical, the vital, the mental, that of knowledge, the blissful. Now in between the physical body and the pranic body there is the subtle-physical. It is also of matter but of subtle matter which does not have the rigid materiality of the gross physical. This subtle-physical sheath or envelope, as it is expressively called, is part of what Sri Aurobindo calls the circumconscient or environmental conciousness.

This subtle-physical covering acts as a buffer between the individual body-life-mind complex and the external world. It corresponds to what is known as the etheric double in the theosophist parlance. All things from outside the individual frame have first to pass through this barrier. It is largely a formation of nervous character and hence is known as the nervous envelope. It radiates an aura which is visible to the inner sight and at times even to the physical eye when it is not too externally occupied. This aura which looks a surrounding impress of light changes its hue in keeping with the moods of the person concerned.

All contacts from the outer atmosphere have got to penetrate through this envelope before they can find lodging in the system. Whether they are nourishing elements or weakening intrusions, they are filtered through the surrounding wall. If this subtle wall is well knit, strong, negative contacts get automatically repelled; even attacks of epidemics are thrown out. But if it be weak, if there are 'holes' in the wall, then their entry becomes easy.

To keep this nervous envelope strong and resistant one must live in a positive way. A robust, cheerful outlook, a capacity of meeting all circumstances and contacts with a habitual optimism, help to strengthen this protective cover. To be prone to depression, to be always anxious, nervous, fearful, irritable, undermines it. This applies to every one, whether he practises yoga or not. In yoga there are definite ways of fortifying this wall: certain asanas, breathing exercises, faith in the protection of the Divine, self-confidence born of trust in the Grace. One learns not to step out of the circle of protection extended by the Guru.

It must be noted that even if there is this circle of protection around oneself, if the nervous covering is punctured again and again by negative movements in daily life, one is exposed to attacks from outside. The situation even invites the attention of the anti-elements in the environment.

13-8-'87

34

UNIVERSAL PSYCHIC

Corresponding to the individual physical formation there is the universal Matter; so are there the universal Life and universal Mind. Is there also a universal Psychic? This question comes up in view of the specially individual nature of the psychic of each person. The psychic, as we know, is the divine spark growing in each individual into a being, carrying the truth the individual is to manifest. The Real-Idea basing the individual manifestation is instinct in this entity. Besides this personal nature of the psychic, we know that this being is not a part of the gradation of the evolving physical, vital and mental beings on the scale of evolution. It stands behind and supports them in their evolution. It is not subject to the limitations of time and space as the other purushas are.

Still, there is a universal Psychic organised as a world behind the ascending series of evolving worlds. It is the land of Peace to which the departed resort and go into internatal trance of recuperation and assimilation of life-experience. Sri Aurobindo gives a vivid description of this 'World-Soul' in his epic *Savitri*. To quote a few lines:

> Into a wonderful bodiless realm he came,
> The home of a passion without name or voice,
> A depth he felt answering to every height,
> A nook was found that could embrace all worlds,
> ...
> The silent soul of all the world was there:
> ...
> The intimacy of God was everywhere,
> ...
> A constant touch of sweetness linked all hearts,
> The throb of one adoration's single bliss
> In a rapt ether of undying love.
> ...
> Immersed in voiceless internatal trance
> The beings that once wore forms on earth sat there
> In shining chambers of spiritual sleep.

14-8-'87

35

NON-BEING

Non-Being is not No-Being. It does not mean that Being does not exist. It means a state of existence that exceeds all formulations of Being. All the determinations and definitions of the Infinite as a Being are transcended. In other words it is an affirmation of the Infinite to exceed its self-chosen determinations for purposes of manifestation.

What is called Asat in the Upanishad, Non-Existence, is a powerful experience as you ascend in consciousness from the spiritual mind. You come to a state where the widest and the highest modes of being, guna, are beyonded. This is termed nirguna, modeless. This is Nirvana, a gate of entry into the Absolute.

From Nirvana you can proceed upon the negative path; equally you can take the positive path. Sri Aurobindo describes how when he had the realisation of Nirvana while meditating with Lele and all world appeared to him merely as a scene of passing figures and images, he felt that was not the end of the story. He waited in silence. And gradually he experienced the affirmations of the Spirit or Brahman as positive Knowledge, Power, Joy, Splendour etc. It is of course possible to pursue the negative line and arrive at what the Buddhists call Shunya, Void. This is the Buddhist Nirvana, the Chinese Tao. Only the Nirvana of the Buddhist is conceived as empty while the Tao contains everything.

By taking to the affirmative, positive path, you pass from the Many of the Overmind into the One of the Supermind and thence to Sat-Chit-Ananda, the highest manifest Truth of the Absolute.

Sri Aurobindo draws attention to the point that the Buddhist Nirvana is not the same as the Brahmanirvana of the Gita. The latter signifies the release—not the extinction—of all the faculties of being into the freedom of Brahman.

Sri Aurobindo points out, repeatedly, that the Shunya, Void, Zero, that is mentioned in various paths, is not really an empty Nothing. If zero it is, it is a pregnant zero:

> Being collapsed into a pointless void
> That yet was a zero parent of the worlds;
>
> —(*Savitri*)

Behind the Zero is Something:

> The zero covers an immortal face.
>
> —(*Ibid*)

The Upanishad is careful to point out that *asat* is not nothing. For out of *asat, sat* cannot come; out of nothing, nothing can come.

17-8-'87

36

THREE ASPECTS OF BRAHMAN

When the Brahman is self-moved to manifest, he reveals himself in three aspects, each of them basing a particular poise of the creative Consciousness. There is, first the Atman, Self, which constitutes the bedrock of the manifestation. The Self stands behind. as it were, and supports each manifestation. In truth it is not only behind, but also within and above—upholding the Form in all ways. The Self, it may be noted, is not only individually poised. It is also universal. But both the individual Self and the universal Self are the same, thus providing the base for the Unity of All.

The Self is impersonal, standing aloof, as it were, from the movement. But on that account it is not static. It has a dynamic aspect also and this truth of the Self manifests as Power.

In each individual movement the Brahman manifests as the Purusha, Person who presides over the activity of nature. Normally this Purusha is enslaved in the rounds of nature, Prakriti. But as his consciousness grows, the Purusha learns to detach himself from nature, stand as a witness and then—if he chooses—function as the master. This Purusha projects himself on the various levels of the being, physical, vital and mental and functions as the purusha of the corresponding gradation of nature.

If the Purusha is the master of the individual nature, Prakriti, the Ishvara is the Lord of the universal Nature. He is the Lord of all. In the consciousness of Ishvara, what is Prakriti at other levels, reveals herself as the Shakti, the Conscious-Power that effectuates his Will. She is the *devātma-shakti* of the Upanishad.

It may be noted that while Mayavada ultimately cancels both the Ishvara and the Purusha, Buddhism does away with the Atman too.

18-8-'87

37

DESTINY NOT INVARIABLE

There is a considerable misunderstanding about destiny. It is held that karma is binding and fate which is an accumulation of the stream of karma is unchanging, unavoidable. In theory this may be admitted. But we forget that this is a world of possibilities. Ours is no world of certainties. Between the sowing of the seed and the expected sprouting, anything can intervene. New possibles may enter into the scene and their effect may be to divert the line of results or even to cancel it.

This becomes possible because there is not one destiny. The individual forges a destiny for himself by his actions. But he does not live alone. He is a member of a family and there is such a thing as family karma, family destiny. This gets mixed up with the individual's. There is also the destiny of the society in which the family lives. The destiny of the society is bound up with the destiny of the country. Thus there are several layers of destiny which influence each other, interact amongst themselves.

That is one side of the matter. Even in the case of the individual, he is a multiple being. His physical destiny is distinct from his vital destiny, mental destiny, and—most important—from his spiritual destiny. Different karmic forces operate in his life and there is a good deal of dilution, mutual cancelling, overriding action of any one of them which is the most powerful. It is possible to offset the results of a karma forged on the physical level by changing the level of one's consciousness. He moves into the orbit of another destiny. This is what happens when the individual takes to spiritual life. He is no more fully bound by the karma of his previous mundane life. Of course it depends upon how far he leaves his past behind and opens himself to a new factor in his life. He may open himself to the action of Grace which is known to wipe out the past karma to a great extent. Or he may create another destiny by his spiritual exertions which could obviate the effects of past karma.

Thus the scope to change one's destiny is large and real. Of course we do not speak here of what is called ineluctable destiny which has got to be worked out for it affects certain fundamental laws of existence.

It goes without saying that as long as one remains on the level where his fate has been shaped, he is subject to that fate. To change it or cancel it, he has to go beyond it—either inward or upward. The choice is his: to let the destiny rule or to surpass it. As Sri Aurobindo puts it,

> Man can accept his fate, he can refuse.
>
> —(*Savitri*)

20-8-'87

38

BHAKTI AND MORALITY

Bhakti, devotion, is a movement of the human towards the Divine. It may be motivated, *sahaituki*, or motiveless, *ahaituki*. As things go, the movement starts usually on some significant occasion in life. One may be saved from danger at a critical moment; the heart wells up in gratitude to the Saviour. One may need something and it comes without trying for it; here again a thanksgiving follows. Such are some of the starting points for the formation of devotion. We do not speak here of devotion arising from fulfilment of prayers. Whatever the occasion or the reason, devotion is essentially a movement of the soul. It may be—and usually is—deformed in the surface being. Mostly it centers itself in the desire-self. But if the person is a little more advanced in his evolution, it becomes a movement in the emotional being.

Though in many cases, the character of this Bhakti retains its primitive character for a long time—even a life-time—, at some point it sheds its pragmatic feature and develops into a spontaneous flow of the being, without any expectation in the mundane sense. A spiritual movement may use it for its motor-power.

The Divine admits both the types of Bhakti, with motive or without. The Divine is not concerned with the moral or the intellectual worth of the person who offers his devotion. Bhakti is independent of social considerations; it is not subject to standards of morality erected by the society. It is a personal movement and all that is needed for Bhakti to be acceptable to the Divine is the sincerity behind it. An unlettered man offering his worship, though totally ignorant of sastras and their injunctions, reaches the Lord directly on the strength of his Bhakti. Another person may not conform to the commonly accepted standards of ethics—social or individual, religious or cultural—and yet his devotion for the Divine may be intense and heart-warming. The Divine is not going to ask him to first shed his 'sins' and coat himself with 'virtues' before his call is heard.

Bhakti stands by itself, true love forms by itself.

They are projections of the soul which is not concerned with extraneous considerations like man-made laws or conventions. Whatever be the starting point, Bhakti, as it grows, lifts the being above all *gunas* and at its best, it melts the human personality into the Divine Person. 21-8-'87

39

COMMUNICATIONS FROM VITAL WORLDS

Quite a number of people receive or seek 'messages' from across the border, from the spirit-world as they say. This world, however, is not of one type. The lowest of these is the region inhabited by spirits that belong to that world and also by disembodied spirits when they leave the earth-zone. Communication with this world is usually through mediums or through automatic writing. Men have claimed that they have spoken to their dead relatives, ancestors, and even to illustrious figures of history. While there may be some element of truth in these claims, mostly it is mischievous spirits pretending to be the wanted persons that play the joke.

There are worlds higher up that are more organised —the vital worlds. Here too there are the lower and the higher vital worlds; there are benevolent beings and malevolent ones. Some of them act on our world, with or without intercession from the human end. Even today there are some in the West who 'receive' whole books at dictation. They are on all kinds of subjects, mainly of a religio-mystic type with a dash of prophecy. They fascinate the gullible and even become the gospels of semi-mystic or occultist schools.

Obviously these messages, however attractive and appealing to certain types of people, are not generally authentic. They are mixed and cannot be relied upon. It depends upon the character of the beings who feature in these interchanges. If they are of a higher order, benevolent beings, their influence can be constructive and helpful, though in the long run they prove to be a barrier for true spiritual development.

Even when these beings are of dubious nature, men can derive benefit in small matters from them. They demand worship, loyalty; in return they will satisfy your petty desires. They will cure illnesses, bring about promotions in life. But their aim is not only to keep their hold on you, but act through you for extending their domain on earth. They mean to possess you completely, wipe out your individuality, push out your soul if they can. These are what are called *kshudra devatas* in the Tantra, wayside deities who insist upon propitiation by sacrifices of animals and other ghastly practices.

How to enter into these vital worlds? It needs considerable occult training and practice under the guidance of an adept. Of course some are born with that capacity. What is insisted upon is that you must have a strong, pure, vital. If the vital is pure, the chances of being misled are few; there is an automatic rejection of wrong influences and contacts.

Indeed, most of us wander into these worlds in dreams but that is involuntary. Our vital being goes into action and we do all kinds of movements which are impossible in our waking state. We fly, we fight with tigers, we give blows to huge beings who dwindle away at our confident stroke. These are no fantasies. They are true happenings in the vital worlds which we

may or may not remember in their fullness when we wake up.
22-8-'87

40

JAPA *vs.* REMEMBRANCE

Are they not the same, Japa and *smarana*, remembrance? Does not Japa automatically involve remembrance of the Divine? Not necessarily, at any rate in the way Japa is usually done. Japa, repetition of the Name, is done verbally, whether audible or not. Even when something within takes up the repetition, it is more or less mechanical. The rest of the being may be engaged in its several pursuits. It may not participate in the act of Japa.

In remembrance the mind plays an active role. It recalls the Divine again and again, whether as a Person or as a Presence or both. When the mind is engaged in this exercise, the heart, the feeling, joins. There is a warmth in the being. The remembrance is not local. It is not confined to the mind. Man is a mental being and the mental consciousness pervades the rest of his being. What the mind thinks or feels has an instant effect on the other parts. That is how remembrance communicates itself to his whole being. It acts as a solvent in as much as it is a conscious process and therefore it wields a power of its own. When the remembrance of the Divine is active there is an almost physical awakening in the being. The emotional parts heave up and currents of devotion, adoration, love spread out from the heart region. The higher vital too responds and imparts its characteristic intensity to the movement. Even the physical has its way of responding. It thrills and there is a palpable sense of involvement. All in all remembrance has a powerful effect on the being. It awakens what is asleep. It speeds up what is slow. It keeps the movement of sadhana alive and growing.

Indeed, both Japa and remembrance can be joined. But the base is *smarana*. Japa is more fruitful when it is a part of the larger movement. Remembrance does not depend upon Japa. It is caused by some need in the being to link itself with the Divine. There is a recall and a reliving of the contact. It may be the Form that comes to life. It may be the Presence that is tangibly felt around oneself. In an instant everything changes. Even the internal circulation of energies is effected. If there has been agitation, a quieting settles down. If things have been dull, there is a quickening. The outlook changes.

In the beginning the movement of remembrance may be intermittent. But as the consciousness weds itself, more and more, to the Ideal, remembrance tends to be more and more effortless. It is on its way to becoming natural and constant. The key is sincerity. The central being must want the Divine as the first need.
23-8-'87

41

DUTY—PROMISE

There are duties and duties. Duty to the family, duty to the class to which one belongs, duty to the country, duty to humanity, and above all duty to one's Self, that is to the Divine. The classic instance of conflict between these different duties is that of Arjuna: whether to kill his kinsmen as a duty-bound Kshatriya or to abstain from slaughter of elders as a responsible member of the family? This was the dilemma he was faced with at the most crucial moment of his life. This was apart from the ethical aspect of the situation: whether it was right to enjoy a blood-stained kingdom after killing endless number of human beings. The right solution has been given by the Divine himself in human form —Sri Krishna. Give up all dharmas (duties) in favour of your duty to the Lord of the Universe. The spiritual is the highest duty for the awakened man.

It is in this light that we have to understand the flexible nature of the compulsion of duty. Usually duty is a clever disguise for self-interest. Even otherwise, if it is something that devolves on man from his station in life, it is binding only as long as he remains in that station. A patriot—in the usual nationalistic sense—may have to give preference to the larger interests of humanity on occasions. Similarly if there be a higher call on his being, the call of the Spirit, he is justified in leaving the lower dharma, duty to the family, to the society etc. in favour of his duty to his Maker. His station in life changes; his consciousness moves in a different dimension requiring him to follow a higher duty.

The same with 'promise' which is governed by the sense of duty. A promise is made under a certain set of conditions, in a particular setting of one's station in life. If that order of life undergoes a change, if one moves into a different context—individual or collective—then the old promise is no longer binding. Indeed, from the point of view of ethics a promise is an undertaking to be honoured under all circumstances. But that is to take too narrow a view of the movement of life which is full of changing, new, demands on man. Not only do promises get out of date, they may even turn suicidal.

The legend of the two promises of Dasaratha and the disasters that followed are a standing warning. As long as a promise is made with an honest intention of fulfilling it, one is entitled to leave it in the flow of life if new conditions necessitate it in the higher interests of the situation. The social or ethical law is no longer relevant to one who places himself under the rule of the spiritual law.
24-8-'87

42

VOICES

It was years ago. A visitor who had come for the Darshan of Sri Aurobindo and the Mother was on his way to the audience. Suddenly he heard a voice: "You are a special personality, you are welcome." Naturally it was a very welcome message and we may be certain he lapped it up. It is needless to say that when this was reported to Sri Aurobindo there was no confirmation. The whole tenor of the words was so alien to Sri Aurobindo.

Such voices abound in the mystic or spiritual sphere. People hear these voices unexpectedly. Some are highly flattering to the ego and tend to be readily accepted. Some are misleading, some threatening. There are voices and voices. They come from all kinds of sources. There are some which emanate from one's own physical or vital or mental being. They are not from any higher region. Hidden desires, preferences, ambitions prompt such voices, especially if the person is vulnerable. The sadhaka is advised to be doubly careful with these voices. They may be from the inner being. Even then they need not be true. For the subliminal—which is the total inner being—shares in the universal Ignorance and is open to error.

Indeed there are voices that guide aright. Usually they come from some higher beings who know more than the human being and can warn or urge with benefit to the recipient. If one is lucky to come into contact with such a being or is chosen by a benevolent source, things go smoothly. One has only to refer and the response is sure. This usually works well in external life but its value is limited in the inner life.

At times some sadhaks who are very sincere in their pursuit are exposed to another kind of voice. It is the voice of the occult critic referred to as *nida* in the Veda. This self-appointed critic takes upon itself to point out to you your imperfections at every step. If you tend to be satisfied with what you have done, for instance, this voice steps forward to tell you that some things are still left undone, that you could have done better. As long as this critic points out the lacunae in your effort and helps in perfecting yourself, it is all very well. But very often this 'censor' exceeds its brief and throws negative suggestions all the while, breaking your morale in the process. One has to be on guard against these interferences.

On the whole, it is safer not to give credence to these voices. For mostly they are from one's own hidden sources. They may be also from agencies that take pleasure in misleading the credulous. The true voice from a diviner source is rare. It requires utmost purity in the being to be open to it and receive it without dilution. Or there must be an intimacy of relation, in which case the Voice of the Deity or the Guru comes through letting no room for doubt or hesitation. It carries the authentic ring.

25-8-'87

43

ATTITUDE IN SADHANA

It is now an accepted axiom in modern psychology that a positive attitude to life helps to make things easier to live with. When we look at events and circumstances with a faith that there is a Providence that guides in the long run and therefore what happens is for our ultimate good, the brighter side of life preponderates over the darker in our vision and experience. Even when the going is hard, we know it is only a phase and that at the end of the tunnel is light. Such an attitude builds a cheerful outlook which is healthy for ourselves and for those who live with us.

If, on the other hand, we are always prone to be negative, we develop into pessimists. We tend to look at everything from a twisted angle and we either exaggerate the unpleasant features or imagine them when in fact there are none. Our whole approach is soured. If this attitude is allowed to develop, there is even a perversion of mind: not only we expect things to go wrong, but secretly we wish them to do so—especially when we are not personally involved. We become cynics. And, as the Mother says, cynicism is the death of spiritual life.

For it strikes at the root of faith. In spiritual life faith in the Divine is a must. The sadhaka recognises a supreme Divine Will and submits himself to it. Whatever takes place, he knows it is permitted by the Divine and he also knows that eventually it contributes to the Purpose. Indeed, it is not enough if it is only a mental attitude. The mind may understand and intellectually accept a certain attitude. But unless it is shared by the other parts of the being, it is not likely to help in shaping his inner life. The emotional being, the vital and even the physical have their samskaras and they have to be educated in accepting the attitude which the mind knows to be right. The emotions go berserk each time anything goes counter to their choice, whatever the approach of the mind be. Similarly the vital overpowers with its push and forces its way despite the disapproval of the mind. It is hardest with the physical. Being nearer the inconscient, it is deeply rooted in inertia and looks upon every change as a threat. It has a poor opinion of the wisdom of the mind. It casts its long shadow on the workings of the mind and influences its attitudes in 'practical' matters.

It is a sadhana by itself to get these parts of the being to accept and share in the attitude of a healthy mind. It takes long. But if the will is strong, they fall in line and there is sunshine.
27-8-'87

44

MORALITY AND LIFE

Standards of morality differ from society to society, from age to age. They change with the state of evolution of the peoples. They are not fundamental laws governing the course of life. Nature itself is amoral. If we look dispassionately at the order of life below the human stage, we do see that morality—as we understand it—does not obtain at those levels. The rule of life that is natural there is described as *matsya nyāya*, logic of the fish: bigger fish swallowing the smaller. Life feeds upon life. Nobody blames the tiger for devouring the deer. The tiger does not become sinful when it kills.

The notion of sin, the formulation of ethics, begins with the arrival of man, the mental being. Standards of morality develop as the human societies form. They become necessary for the well-being of human collectivities in as much as they restrain the unbridled egoism and vital aggression that are prominent features of human evolution at primitive stages. The concept of sin is also a contribution of the mind, more or less to keep the vital instincts in check.

The world at large does not run on lines of moral laws. More fundamental laws e.g. evolution, karma, growth of consciousness etc. are the main laws on which the life-movement proceeds. A stage does come in the life of the awakened individual when he naturally transcends the values of morality and governs his life on the higher basis of spiritual truths. But on that account it does not mean that he acts immoral. We may say he is super-moral.

Thus morality is a necessary aid at some stage in the collective evolution of humanity, in order to humanise man, discard the animal elements inherited from the past. It is no more relevant once man does not need its regulation for his higher evolution. He discards the crutch.

28-8-'87

45

SUICIDE A CRIME

Despite all talk of the right of the individual to end his life if he chooses to do so, the fact remains that the act of suicide is a crime. It is a triple crime: against God, against Nature, against one's own self.

Life is given by the Divine for a purpose. It is a double purpose, to further the individual evolution and to participate in the universal manifestation. By defeating this purpose by self-destruction, one commits an offence against the Divine.

Nature expends so much of energy and care in bringing a person to life. This labour in shaping a complex system like the human is deep and intricate. Nature intends to work out her scheme of effectuating the will of the Creator through such carefully designed instruments. To deprive her of the fruit of her exertions by interfering with her course is criminal.

And it is an irreparable denial of the truth of one's own being. Each person is an embodiment of a soul with all its powers and potentialities. The soul comes to this earth in order to grow in experience of life and add to its stature in consciousness growing towards the parent Divine. It comes with a long preparation for a set objective. By wanton self-destruction, one defeats one's self. It is a cruel, thoughtless cutting short of a precious innings in the evolution of the soul.

Furthermore, suicide is pointless. It achieves nothing. Rather it puts back the clock and adds more difficulties to the situation. The person who is drawn to this unnatural step thinks that he would escape the difficulties that confront him in life by walking away from it. He imagines he can cheat life. But what follows the act of self-undoing is the reverse. He is obliged to face the very same difficulties in the after-world but with this difference that there is no more the fortress of the physical body in which to function. He is all at sea, at the mercy of every mocking element. He repents, he curses himself, but there is no way out. He has to suffer for the wrong he has done, the heinous crime he has committed.

And that is not the end of the story: to suffer in the after-death condition. When he comes back to earth-life, as he has to, he is faced with the very same difficulties to avoid which he had run away. Run away, yes. For it is an act of cowardice to slink away from the challenges of life by the backdoor. The soul insists upon going through the experience it had chosen in the previous life that was cut short. Once again the situation is the same, perhaps worse.

Suicide solves no problem. It is an offence against God, interference with Mother-Nature, betrayal of the divine self at the heart of the individual.

46

PAST MISTAKES

Every one does mistakes. Some out of ignorance and some out of habit. There are still others who know it is wrong and yet commit it. As the consciousness develops and one becomes aware of the distinction between right and wrong, there is often a sense of guilt and tendency to brood over it. This happens particularly with those whose moral sensibilities get keen or who take to spiritual life.

At some stage in their sadhana there is an upsurge of all the past memories—often exaggerated in their dimensions. One recalls the wrongs one has done to others in the past, relives the scenes and is filled with remorse. If this movement is indulged in it assumes frightening proportions and one is consumed with sadness, self-deprecation. It may even develop into a complex. This is a pitfall to be guarded against.

What is the way out? The truth of the matter is that once one realises the mistake or wrong one has done at any point of time, and feels contrite, a forward step is registered. One regrets, one repents; that is the first stage. The next is to take a decision not to repeat the same movement of the past in future. There must be a will to desist from such acts. In the measure of the sincerity with which one repents and decides not to allow the past movement to recur, the karma of that action loses its hold, if it does not cease altogether. If one believes in the Divine, it helps to pray for forgiveness and strength to desist from the offending movement in similar circumstances.

Thereafter one should not recall or dwell on the past. To do so prolongs the old vibrations in the consciousness and opens the door to depressions. It may even develop into a habit leading to a permanent damage to the psyche. One must refuse to relive the past even negatively.

2-10-'87

47

WITHDRAWAL

One of the common wrong notions about spiritual life is that by withdrawing from the world of action and going into some kind of retreat, one makes a definitive entry into the Quest for God. Instances are plenty of persons giving up their responsibilities in life and going into seclusion for pursuing their path to the chosen goal. But this is hardly the solution.

Mere withdrawal from life in the world is not the key. Usually one carries his world wherever he goes. Often that world weighs more heavily at the psychological level in the absence of the pressures of daily activity. One tends to live in a subjective realm which can develop into dangerous fantasy. Besides, the seeds of attachments and desires remain beneath the surface. They erupt at the first opportunity and the sadhaka is caught unawares. Just to withdraw from the scene of temptations and distractions does not mean that the bonds have been snapped. He needs to work upon them, patiently, meticulously. In a sense it is harder to overcome these impediments in solitude than in the midst of life where there are tests galore to let him know how far he has succeeded in releasing himself from those knots. It is easy to imagine that he is free from them as long as there are no provocations. But Nature will not let anyone stay long in complacency. In one way or other the man is put to test. Legends in the Puranas of austere ascetics succumbing to the first temptation are not just stories for edification. They are warnings.

Again, withdrawal without a discipline to rise out of the usual mental consciousness into a higher spiritual consciousness has no value. The sadhaka must utilise the opportunities of solitude for intensive self-observation, self-correction and replacement of mental values by the spiritual. Even if he learns to stand aloof from the customary actions and reactions of life, he only forms a neutral attitude. That is not enough. He needs to develop a spiritual dynamism. Indeed, temporary withdrawals may be necessary for working out these changes in himself, but they cannot be for all time. As the Mother says, the real progress is made in the midst of the challenges of life, not away from the scene.

Of course this cannot be made an absolute rule. For some it may be necessary to go into solitude in order to work out and establish new states of consciousness. Even in such cases, the withdrawal is only in appearance. They do keep their links with the world in a subtle manner and let their spiritual gains seep into the general life. Their withdrawal is only a strategic one, not a complete divorce from life in the world. The physical is, after all, not the only level of life.

A note of warning may be usefully added here. Very often the urge to cut off from 'people', cease talking to all and sundry, shut oneself into some sort of seclusion, opens the door to all kinds of subjective movements of an egoistic and vital character. The original intention of speeding up the spiritual progress is covered up and wrong turns are taken. Instances are galore of persons who have succumbed to such temptations, getting unbalanced. Sri Aurobindo had to warn repeatedly against such misadventures.
12-10-'87

48

BRAHMIC CONSCIOUSNESS

Thanks to the Gita (Chap. 2), we have a fair idea of what the Brahman Consciousness is. The first experience of this state is one of imperturbable Calm and great Peace. There is a solid Silence in the mind. But this is not all. As the experience deepens itself or enlarges itself, there is also the movement of strong Power, Action, welling out of the established Silence and Peace. The Brahmic Consciousness embraces both: static poise as well as dynamic activity.

Naturally this state does not come about all of a sudden. The sadhaka becomes aware of its presence on the heights or in the depths of his being, in the course of his meditations or other yogic practices. At first they may be glimpses. Gradually, however, in response to his aspiration and persistence, the state lasts for a while. He learns to contact this Consciousness in his high moments. By practice he acquires the capacity to go there at will. Or it may happen that this state reflects itself in his mind or in the deeper parts of his being. All these are steps to a greater and stabler realisation: to be able to reach and stay there.

When he is thus established in this Consciousness there is a permanent calm and peace in his being. He is not touched by the prevailing dualities of life. At the most they may brush on his surface nature, but they leave no mark on his being. He fronts all contacts in an impersonal way. He has no likes or dislikes. He is neither elated nor depressed; he takes things as they come.

But on that account he is not devoid of initiative or impulse to action. He does act, but from another level than the common. He acts as he is moved. And because the source of his action is outside the range of personal ego and desire—they have long ceased to exist for him—he is more effective. Indeed, his activity may not be always visible on the physical plane. He functions more on subtler levels and produces more lasting results in the collectivity of which he is a member.

Usually this Consciousness descends in the mind. The surface agitations subside and the mind is able to reflect the movements of higher faculties beyond the intellect. It perceives deeper, beyond appearances. When, however, in the process of yoga, this Consciousness descends into the vital, there is likely to be a great commotion, unless the vital has been sufficiently purified before. At the impact of the spiritual peace and the touch of the impersonal, the vital which is always prone to ceaseless activity and personal satisfaction gets alarmed and disturbances ensue. Hidden impulses rush up and create havoc. All kinds of suppressed desires, ambitions spring up to seize the Power that comes along with the higher Consciousness and drive the practitioner on a perilous course. Here is the breeding ground of *yoga-bhrashthas*.

13-10-'87

49

DESCENT

The concept of ascent of consciousness is ancient. The Veda speaks repeatedly of 'rising' to the world of Light, reaching the realm of Gods in the Home of Truth. The Tantra has familiarised us with the phenomenon of the rising of the inner potential—Kundalini—from its basal centre to the crown of the head. There are other systems of yoga combining the principles of both the traditions—Veda and Tantra—in which the movement of ascent figures prominently. We do not speak at the moment of still another way, the technique of interiorisation in which one plunges inward in quest of the Reality. Focussing on the route upward, we note that ascent of consciousness is a must in paths that follow the evolutionary course of Nature.

At every stage in the history of evolution of the world, there has been a marked ascent of the concealed conscious-force to higher and higher levels of existence. This is aptly described in the Tantra as *ārohana*, climbing up. But corresponding to this ascent is a descent, *avarohana*, of what is above. Each step of the ascending movement acts as a call to what stands above to descend. And, we must note, that this descent plays a greater role in the whole movement. It is the descent that brings in new elements in the situation at our level. Without this fresh ingression at each step, we would be turning in circles. The impact of the higher and newer factors leads to a leap of what is lower. It exerts pressure. It also opens the way for further ascents. Thus while the initial impulse is caused by the ascent of aspiration, the ensuing results follow on the heels of the descent in response. Things are made easier. Obstructions are removed by a force from a higher level.

Each descent releases something that is involved below and the upward movement is speeded up. Legends of heavenly Rivers rushing down and sweeping away obstinate rocks on earth—physical and psychological—are symbolic of this action of higher Nature in transforming the lower. There is a stage in sadhana when the main emphasis is on purification and ascent of aspiration in the being. This is only a preparation for the next step which is a descent of what is aspired for. It helps if a state of receptivity and silence is built up so that there is no interference in the movement of descent, no dilution.

15-10-'87

50

EGO-HABIT

In saying "The ego was the helper, the ego is the bar", Sri Aurobindo sums up all that can be said about this ubiquitous element in every evolutionary being, notably man. For the ego has been a deliberate contrivance of Nature to focuss the life-movements around a central point in the being. As such it has served a capital role in individuating the evolving consciousness. But a stage has now arrived, at the human level, when it has become a road-block for further advance. It is preventing the emergence of the true centre and giving a wrong turn to the growing consciousness of man. That is why all spiritual disciplines insist on eliminating the ego.

But this is easier said than done. For the ego-formation is not just on the surface nature. It is entrenched deep on all levels of the being and the vital element in it is very cunning. Persons who think they have got over the ego find themselves suddenly confronted by an ego-movement in a deceptive form. There are enough movements in life that have an idealist colour but hide strong egoism underneath. Virtues, altruism, learning, are some of the cloaks that conceal a flourishing ego.

Even when a person is sincere in getting rid of egoism, the sense of 'I' and 'Mine' in day-to-day life, and takes steps to weed it out from his motivations and activities, the game is not over. He may not be overtly egoistic. But without his being aware of it the head of ego peeps in here and there. It is easier for others to spot out the offender. The ego-habit in nature, particularly rajasic nature dies hard. This is particularly seen in the case of those who are convinced that they are free from ego but have habit of seeing the ego in others. The Mother once remarked that it is those who have a strong ego in themselves that complain of ego in others.

It takes time even for one who is sincere in his resolve to leave the ego behind. Meanwhile it is useful to know some of the signs of the ego on its way out. The stress of individuality diminishes. More and more of impersonality is established in the being. Likes and dislikes, preferences and prejudices, fade out. The centre of reference in daily life is not oneself but the Divine, whether as the Individual Divine or the Universal. There is a shift of consciousness from the personal to a deeper or higher centre. Reactions and responses no longer proceed from the personal angle.

No doubt it is a hard way and the ego-habit long established in nature buts in now and then. Vigilance and transparent sincerity are the only safeguards. There is a more positive way and that is to open to the action of the psychic. When the psychic is active, the ego or even the shadow of ego has little chance to show up. The being feels it vulgar and there is an automatic rejection of the movement.
16-10-'87

51

PHOTOGRAPH MOVES

Time and again devotees are overtaken by amazement at pictures of Gods or Gurus whom they worship, moving. Perhaps it is a subjective phenomenon, observe some of them. But most are obliged to dismiss the doubt because their experience has been so vivid.

It is not uncommon for those who visit the Reception Room in our Ashram and gaze at the famous Photograph of Sri Aurobindo, to find the figure moving. It may advance towards them. More common is the experience of devotees with the Mother's calender pictures. As we all know, each year a fresh picture is issued on the calendar—lovely, bewitching photo-print. Many have been astonished by a sudden smile on the face. Some see it moving. Is it all imagination? or wishful sight?

It is not. Many of these pictures are charged with the Presence of the original. The Mother once observed that each photograph of hers has captured her particular state of consciousness at the moment. And that consciousness, the power of that consciousness, is always active. How far it impacts on us depends upon our own condition, receptivity, communication at each time. Even regarding Idols or Images of Deities, the devotion and sincerity of the worshipper plays a large part in activising the power, prana, in them. In the absence of such invoking vibrations, there is usually no articulation. Visibly active or not, the Presence is there.

It will be clear in this context how there is a truth in the response of Grace through the falling of a flower from the body of the Deity. This is no superstition. Events have confirmed it again and again.

We must note, in this connection, that negative indications also come true in most cases. Someone takes a flower-offering. But in the act of giving, the flower falls down, the fruit rolls over. This usually indicates some defect in the approach of the person or is an advance intimation that the purpose which he has in mind is not likely to be served. They call these omens. Of course it is possible, to a great extent, to treat them as warnings and invoke the Divine Grace to avert the possible dangers. It is a question of how far one is vigilant and trustful in the protective Grace.

There are good omens and bad omens. How far one should let them influence one's life is another matter which merits separate treatment.

24-10-'87

52

DESIRE AND LIBERATION

All liberated beings are not alike. Some are childlike and move us with the innocence of their nature. Some are inert, allergic to movement; they want to be left alone wherever they are. Some are always 'high', intoxicated as it were. Always intense and taut in their reactions, they are unpredictable; they may fly at you for any reason or no reason. There are some others who are disorderly, crude and even disgusting. All of these types are different in their behaviour; the only common denominator is their state of liberation. They are perpetually in a state of luminous union with the Self. But that is an inner condition. It has little effect on their outer nature which continues to follow its old pattern. There is no equilibrium between their inner and outer states.

Thus one may continue to have desires and yet be liberated within. This is possible for in most of the yogas the external nature, prakriti, is left to itself. All effort, concentration, is on realising the Self within. The plunge inwards to the individual Self or outwards to the universal Self is one-pointed. The outer nature is ignored or kept out of attention. It is taken for granted that this nature will always be what it has been, incorrigible. It is waste of effort to seek to change it. Thus it is that one often finds glaring contradictions in some of the obviously liberated persons. What happens to the old nature, its unexhausted desires for example? The desires die with the death of the body. Isolated as they have been from the inner being, during life-time, they cannot continue after the cessation of bodily life.

Naturally this course is not open to the seeker of the integral path. For him the inner liberation into identity with the Self is not the end. It is, so to say, the first capital step towards an integral liberation which very much includes the recasting of nature in terms of the inner liberation. Otherwise it remains a partial achievement. He has to work for and establish harmony between the inner state and the outer so that the external life becomes a faithful mirror of the luminous condition within.
25-10-'87

53

ON HEALING

There are different types of healing: physical healing, psychological healing and the spiritual. There is further long-distance healing and healing by touch. In all these there is an interaction between the person who heals and the healed. The sources of the healing operation are also different. Largely it is the vital energy of the healer that is directed into the patient; this helps the vital force in the body to flow with additional strength and set right the disorder. The healer has either an abundant fund of vitality in himself or he can link himself to the ocean of vital energies in the universe and draw from it for his purpose. In spiritual healing, it is the higher spiritual force that is brought into the situation. While the results of the augmentation of the vitality tend to be temporary, those of spiritual action are more lasting; for the spiritual power emanates from a higher or deeper source which is nearer the bases of harmony and truth.

Whatever the nature of the healing, the patient must have faith. He should have faith in the capacity of the healer to help, faith in the power that is set to act in him. This faith plays a capital role in bringing about the desired results. It uses the external agency as an instrument to correct the disturbance. That is why it is often said that in most cases it is faith that cures. Faith is power of the soul and it is self-effective. Under proper conditions it can cure by itself, even without external aid. Even if it is not strong, it is used as a fulcrum for action by the healing Power.

Is faith indispensable? Can healing not be done in the absence of faith? It is possible, says Sri Aurobindo. Only the person concerned—the patient—should not know that he is being acted upon. In the absence of opposition or interference by his surface being, particularly his mind, the healing force acts directly upon his subliminal and taps the inner reservoir. Health-giving forces are released and the cure effected. The person who is thus cured may not know at all how his health has returned. Decidedly a subject with faith who collaborates with the physician—here a healer—is the best bet. But a person who does not know offers his own advantages; his personality has little or no chance to interfere or dilute.

27-10-'87

54

IMPOSED DISCIPLINE

It is a question that has often come up in our Ashram: Has a discipline imposed from outside real value in the evolution of man? The Mother did not believe in rules and regulations in a society of seekers. She emphasised rather on an inner discipline voluntarily practised by the sadhaka. She even said that she had no value for a change brought about by pressure from outside.

While this position is understandable in an environment like a collectivity aspiring to develop into a spiritual society, doubts are raised regarding the commonalty of humans. It may be readily conceded that as long as one is not awakened to the call of spiritual destiny, ethical and social norms are indispensable. They subdue the the lower movements of nature and train the being to discriminate between the wholesome and the unwholesome ways of living. One may or may not understand the deeper principles underlying the codes of conduct. Still they have a refining and purifying effect.

Even in the case of sadhakas, Sri Aurobindo points out, external regulations have a beneficial role. The seekers must first understand the aim of these requirements and voluntarily submit themselves to them. They do profit in the measure of their sincerity. Naturally they do not treat these as compulsive impositions but as helpful aids in their spiritual endeavour. For them it is not so much the letter as the spirit of the injunctions that is important.

Speaking of inner discipline, it can be practised only by those who are sufficiently mature in consciousness and feel the need for change. They do not need external reminders to be on the right side. Reminders are useful only to those who still have parts in their nature that respond to lower excitations in life. In other words they have a role to play in the case of those who are not yet singly committed to the spiritual ideal. For a practising sadhaka the inner compulsions are such that external impositions are redundant, they are relics of the past.

Thus it is for each individual to face the truth and see for himself whether he needs directions and proddings from outside or he is developed enough to respond to an active inner sense of what is right and what is wrong in each situation. Imposed discipline is good as long as it is necessary. A stage arrives—or should arrive—when it becomes artificial and stands in the way of spontaneous growth of the inner being.
27-10-'87

55

REALISATION OF ONE IN ALL

Most of the spiritual traditions are concerned with individual salvation. Techniques are evolved and perfected to help the seeker in effecting his liberation from nature or karma and subsequent emergence into the freedom of the Spirit. Whether the goal is positive as in the Vedantic sadhanas or negative as in most of the Buddhist paths, the character of the effort is severely individual. In fact there is a studied attempt to cut oneself off from the general life-movement which is left to itself as incorrigible.

There are, however, a few brave spirits who make it their life-mission to work for the progressive liberation of the world in its entirety. They do not stop with their personal achievement. Indeed, for them that is a capital step enabling them to make a meaningful effort to extend their realisation to others. This becomes possible because of an essential oneness of life in the universe. There is a universal Mind, a universal Vital, a universal

Physical. What takes place at one point in this universal existence, at whatever level, spreads itself to other points, provided that what has happened is sufficiently deep and powerful enough to make a dent in the existing structure.

Thus if one succeeds in establishing the action of Intuition in his mind in an organised way, it creates similar possibilities in other minds. Things become easier for those that follow the same way of opening the mind to the higher power of Intuition. In common language we may say there is a chain reaction, a subtle communication at that level of the new working. Such attempts have been made by the Vedic Rishis, for instance, in the realm of spiritual consciousness. They have, as recorded in their hymns, scaled certain heights of being, established those conquests for the benefit of humanity to come.

Naturally the way one proceeds is different. Where one is content with one's own liberation, there is a certain isolation from the general life. The difficulties are only of individual nature and can be dealt with with persistence of will and hard work. But where the object is to relate one's realisation to the universal existence, naturally things assume a different character. One has then to face the universal Nature which puts up dour opposition to any attempt at changing its established habit. Thus, Sri Aurobindo and the Mother point out that when they deal with the subconscient, it is not just their own individual subconscient that has to be tackled; the encounter is with the general, universal Subconscient. Each step gained in the conquest of the subconscient ranges of oneself is pushed back by a wave from the general Subconscient. The work of opening up the subconscient to the action of the Spirit has to be done at a fundamental level, at the level of the Principle, and therefore it offers enormous difficulties. If, however, the pioneer succeeds in boring through and throws the region open to the higher Light of Truth, then as a consequence the doors are opened to the generality to make a similar breakthrough. This is what is meant by the realisation of one person reaching All.

One man's perfection still can save the world.
(Sri Aurobindo: *Savitri*)

29-10-'87

56

THE ONE THING IN LIFE

Sri Ramakrishna gives the analogy of a fish thrown out of water struggling to get back. It has a sense of suffocation till it finds the water. Similar should be, he says, the seeking of the sadhaka; he has a true call, he is earnest in his practice, only when he is consumed by such an intense longing and cannot do without the Divine even for a moment.

Sri Aurobindo insists that one who is serious about his quest should make it the one thing in his life that matters. This need, aspiration, should form the constant background—and also the foreground—of his daily life. He should keep this urgency all through. Whatever his occupations, the spiritual demand should always stay at the centre of his life. It is not that he should give up other concerns, that he should abstain from all other activity. That is not called for nor is it wholesome. Sadhakas of the integral yoga are expected to carry on whatever activities fall to their share in life. But they must be always subsidiary with the spiritual preoccupation forming the main interest. Furthermore, whatever the other occupations, obligatory or voluntary, in collective life, they must be carried on in the spirit of the spiritual quest. The spiritual must suffuse all of his movements, whether they are thoughts, emotions, impulsions or actions. Each must be related to the central need of the being—to realise the Divine.

Does it not result in tension, impatience, excessive self-concern? It need not and should not. As long as the sadhaka believes he is doing the effort and relies upon his own strength, things may turn in this direction. But if he is wise and recognises that the task is beyond his puny human capability, and lays his burden on the Divine by surrendering himself, there is neither hurry nor tension. He has faith in the Wisdom of the Divine, in the all-effecting Grace of the Divine and he is content to leave the results to the Divine. Of course he does his part of enabling sadhana. He does it in an unhurried manner, sure of each step, conscious of the supporting Power. He makes the spiritual his central objective and organises all else around it. Without it, life loses its meaning for him. Everything is a feeder to the flame on the altar.

30-10-'87

57

WRONG IDEAS OF JUSTICE

It is a common notion that there is a justice operating in this world ensuring that every good deed is rewarded by advancement in material affluence and every bad one punished by misfortune. Maybe this working of justice takes time to effectuate itself; the lollipops and the whip-lashes may arrive in a subsequent birth, but the system is bound to work.

Actualities in life, however, do not appear to support this reading. For we often see the virtuous man loaded with a plethora of difficulties while the wicked man merrily goes on prospering. The popular explanation that the presently virtuous person is paying for some past misdeed and the other one was a paragon of virtue in his last birth, fails to satisfy the rational mind. If, however, we look a little deeper into the facts of life, the situation is somewhat different.

Justice, the Mother observes, is the strict determinism of Nature. For every action there is a corresponding reaction. Each energy expended evokes a corresponding result—true to its type. It has nothing to do with moral or religious considerations. Thus if one exerts himself with all his talents and energies in a venture, he is likely to succeed in his objective. It is irrelevant here whether he is a man of virtue and piety or an unscrupulous person. The results will be commensurate with the effort; there is always a correlation between the type of energies put out and the type of results that ensue.

If, for instance, one lives according to an ethical code, he gains in moral strength. Economic factors do not enter into the situation. Similarly if one practises deceit, falsehood, he is weakened in his moral fibre. The level of his consciousness within sinks down. And from the point of his evolutionary development his clock is put back. His investments may bring in more dividends; that has nothing to do with his faults of character. His financial gains are the result of his exercise of practical intelligence and foresight.

Thus there is a confusion of categories in the popu-

lar mind on this subject. Nature is a diligent accountant and she does not allow a mix-up of transactions. From this point of view justice is what ensures the operation of the law of action and reaction on the same level of functioning. Moral effort leads to moral growth; spiritual effort brings in spiritual progress. It is not permissible to bring in other considerations in the context.
31-10-'87

58

DIVINE CONSCIOUSNESS

What is the content of the divine consciousness? In what precise way does it differ from the ordinary human consciousness? Answering this question, Sri Aurobindo gives a few hints of the changes that come over when the divine consciousness gets established.

In the first place there is a perpetual calm. There is no room for agitation, disturbance, whatever may happen. There is no excitement of any kind. Even in the midst of calamitous happenings the inner calm is not disturbed. It may even look as if the person is callous. But it is not so. On the other hand there is a deep identification and the very calm within has a soothing effect on the surroundings. Vibrations of strength help to stabilise the situation.

That brings us to the next characteristic: strength. There is no room for weakness anywhere in the being. A mastering strength is always there and it gives security to things around. Persons in the environment feel a constant surge of strength. Some may even flatter themselves that the strength is their own. They forget that they are rowing in someone else's boat.

There is no longer any sense of being confined to the body. There is a constant experience of expansion. Actually one lives in the subtle body which is open to Infinity. There is an effortless participation in the vastitude pervading the universe. There are no boundaries to one's existence. Whether within or around or above, there is an endless infinitude. It is something more than cosmicisation. For one lives even in the Beyond.

Side by side, a link is formed with Eternity. The timelessness of the Self within seeps through and through. As one lives more and more in that dimension, the sense of immortality pervades the being. Death of the body ceases to be a threat. For even while living in the physical body, there is always a realisation of existence beyond it. One does not care whether the body lives or dies.

And division ceases to be. There is no longer the oppressive sense of 'other' ness. Everywhere one feels the presence of the Divine. In each form, each individual, one greets the One. In such a setting it is impossible to hate any one, to shrink from any one. For all is Brahman. In the unforgettable language of Sri Aurobindo describing his state, "As I look around this room, I see everything as the Brahman. No, it is not mere thinking, it is a concrete experience. Even the wall, the books are the Brahman. I see you no longer as M. but as the Divine living in the Divine. It is a wonderful experience."

1-11-'87

59

SMELLS

It is not unusual to sense some powerful smell suddenly spreading in the atmosphere. At times it is of jasmine, at times of incense or it is some new kind of fragrance. Occasionally the smell may be of some unwelcome odour. It may be something like kerosene smell. The interesting part of the phenomenon is that not all who are present get the smell. Only one or a few get it. The rest do not experience the smell.

Naturally we test for ourselves whether there is any physical cause for these smells: whether the particular flowers are in the environs or the incense is being burnt somewhere near. When physical verification fails to give any clue and yet the smell is undeniable, we look for an explanation.

The fact is that there is a subtle world looming over our gross material world. Everything here on earth has its corresponding similar on the subtler plane. Thus there are sounds, forms, smells etc. Only they are more intense in their formation. They have a quality that is somewhat unearthly. They are usually more concentrated, more well-defined. Those who practise yoga or any discipline that awakens the hidden faculties in us are likely to experience this phenomenon. The subtler sight or hearing or sense of smell opens in the course of expansion of consciousness and things that properly belong to subtler planes come into the range of the awakened faculties. Thus it is that we may begin to hear the yoga sounds viz. flute notes, ocean waves etc. So too with smells. They testify to the opening of our latent faculties. They are signs of advancement in yoga.

As noted earlier, the smells can be of an unwelcome type too. For one may open to the nether side of the subtle world; some part of nature may open out into the lower regions; and ugly scenes or evil smells may be experienced.

P.S.

A graphic description of the subtle sounds heard in yoga is to be found in Sri Aurobindo's *Savitri*:

> The immortal cry ravished the captive ear,
> Then, lowering its imperious mystery,
> It sank to a whisper circling round the soul.
> It seemed the yearning of a lonely flute
> That roamed along the shores of memory
> And filled the eyes with tears of longing joy.
> A cricket's rash and fiery single note,
> It marked with shrill melody night's moonless hush
> And beat upon a nerve of mystic sleep
> Its high insistent magical reveille.
> A jingling silver laugh of anklet bells
> Travelled the roads of a solitary heart;
> Its dance solaced an eternal loneliness:
> An old forgotten sweetness sobbing came.
> Or from a far harmonious distance heard
> The tinkling pace of a long caravan
> It seemed at times, or a vast forest's hymn,
> The solemn reminder of a temple gong,
> A bee-croon honey-drunk in summer isles
> Ardent with ecstasy in a slumberous noon,
> Or the far anthem of a pilgrim sea.
>
> (II.14)

2-11-'87

60

RIDDING OF EGOISM

It is widely accepted that the ego is inimical to spiritual consciousness. It takes time to get rid of it. In the first place one must become conscious of the play of ego in oneself. More often than not people get offended when it is pointed out to them that they are egoistic. They disclaim it with a vehemence that tells a different tale. The spiritual aspirant must have the humility to recognise that he has the legacy of ego in his nature and he must be vigilant to spot its strains in his daily life. Once he accepts this fact, the next step becomes easier.

It is to dissociate himself from the activities of his nature, prakriti. He learns to take his stand in the purusha within. From that poise he stands outside the streamings of nature; he does not react to contacts and impacts that are part of life in the world. In the measure of his sincerity a gulf is formed between his consciousness as a person and the mechanical activity of his nature. The sense of myness, mine, slowly disappears. As this detachment stabilises itself, the sanction of the purusha comes to be withdrawn from the prakriti; prakriti loses its initiative and hold. A spiritual control takes charge and the ego recedes.

It is also possible to reject the ego-mixed movements before they form themselves. Naturally it is a difficult process, but effective in results. After some time of this vigilant practice, the action becomes automatic. Things are rejected without calling for attention.

There is also a mental control. In effect it is the mind that tries to control the vital. Sri Aurobindo points out that this control is partial and temporary. Things are only suppressed and have a way of erupting. It is disconcerting to find movements that were considered gone rushing up with force, violence. They have only been driven in the subconscient, not thrown out of the system. They await their opportunity which usually arrives when one slides into some inertia or lets the consciousness drop into a spell of unconsciousness.

Till the ego is fully replaced by the psychic, there is always the danger of its showing up. The wise way, therefore, is not to struggle with the ego but to build up the psychic movements in the being.
12-11-'87

61

DON'T DICTATE

One reads in books how in yoga there is a flow of experiences. They may be sounds, visions, dreams of the premonitary kind, flow of honey in the mouth, surge of joy in the heart and so on. Naturally there is a tendency among novices to expect these experiences—some of them if not all—to come their way. If they do not or if there be delay in their appearance, they worry themselves and lament that they are not progressing.

Truth to tell, experiences of the visual or auditory kind are not at all a must. One can go ahead without any of these taking place. What is important is to feel the quietude of mind, peace around oneself. It is more important to feel the Presence than to 'see'. Further the type of experiences that one gets usually depends upon one's nature, temperament and the line of yoga that one pursues. If there is an emphasis on the vital, for instance, which begins at the emotional level, there is likely to be a luxuriance of visions and dramatic interludes. If the approach is mental, the subconscious mind has a way of building up imaginative edifices.

Few of these have any lasting spiritual value. The ideal way to get a stable foothold and step on the path is to keep the being calm. There should be no expectations, no anticipations. At the human end there must be only aspiration and opening to what is aspired for: the Divine Consciousness. One gathers up all energies and focusses them on the object of prayer or meditation. Thereafter one stays silent, leaving the field clear for the working of the Higher Consciousness. When this is done with faith and trust in the guiding Power, the best under the circumstances, the needed movement at the moment, tends to take place. Do not dictate in advance, Sri Aurobindo warns the seeker. If the meditator expects experiences of a particular kind viz. lights, colours, images to appear, he may be disappointed. Or he may be in for what the Mother calls imitative experience. What one strongly wants projects itself before the mind's eye. It has no origin in truth. It is all misleading. Every one need not get the identical experiences that another has. One can progress without any of such spectacular experiences. Someone likened them to fireworks; they make a good deal of noise but come to nothing. Spiritually it is more productive if one is quiet, receptive and observant. If any experience takes place, do not rush at it and treat it as a realisation. That experience is not the final. It may or may not be followed by another. If it holds a significance, note it but do not overvalue it. A true experience with a spiritual origin always leaves some unmistakable effect upon the rest of the being. That effect must be allowed to sink in, stabilise itself. Excitement, hurry to announce, weaken the experience.

It is not that experiences in yoga have no value. They do have when they come unasked, from a deeper or higher source. They indicate, they are milestones on the way. Treat them as such, do not give undue importance to them. Do not look for them, do not stimulate them.

30-11-'87

62

CHOOSING NOT TO KNOW

It is a common superstition that saints and God-realised persons know everything, they are kind of omniscient. Many are the shocks that the faithful receive when they discover that their belief is ill-placed. They find that the Masters do not know everything that happens under the sun. This appears to be strange for the Divine is admittedly omniscient and those who are one with that Consciousness ought to share in that omniscience.

Answering a pertinent question on the matter, relating to the Mother, Sri Aurobindo replied that the Mother knew what she chose to know. She had too much on her hands and she needed to know just what was needed at each moment. She had only to turn her gaze to the situation in question in order to know the truth of the matter.

Speaking on an important occasion in answer to an anxious query by a disciple, the Mother explained that she knew *there* (on a higher level of her consciousness) but not *here* (on the working, day-to-day level). That is understandable.

Further light on the subject is shed by a remark of Sri Aurobindo that it is not always good to know. He explains that if he knew for certain what was going to happen, he would be bound to it, whether he liked it or not. That pre-knowledge would hamper his freedom to handle other possibilities. He preferred to work on the existing possibilities in the direction of his choice, uninfluenced by any foreknowledge. One is fettered in exerting oneself in a given situation if he were to know what was going to happen. He would lose interest in the present. That is why we see many an Avatar functioning from moment to moment.

It is also a fact that in this world of possibles, things can be changed even if they happen to be fixed by some confluence of factors. New factors can be brought into play and the pre-figured destiny transcended. In such an operation, pre-knowledge interferes. Knowledge is deliberately localised and a force built up that upsets an unknown arrangement. We have known instances where the Mother did not want to know what was actually taking place; she pushed that knowledge away from her or pushed it behind. The result was, quite often, settled things were unsettled.

1-12-'87

63

WORKINGS OF THE FORCE

It is common to see entrants in Integral Yoga complaining of headaches during or after meditation. They feel heaviness in the head. And this kind of headache does not yield to aspirin. That is because it is not the usual kind of heaviness. It is a yogic phenomenon in the early stages of sadhana. When the Yoga-Shakti, the higher Force begins to act, there is often some resistence in the being and this makes itself felt as heaviness. The remedy is to relax. In due course the complaint disappears as the system gets used to the new workings. There is an automatic adjustment. It is also advised, on such occasions, to engage oneself in some activity or take a walk, so that there is an easier circulation of energies in the body.

Some experience a more uncomfortable sensation: it is as if some drilling is going on in the head. One has only to bear it, by ignoring it, if possible. The Force works upon certain cells in the brain. There are some who are unable to contain the Force; their bodies sway. This very movement helps, at times, the Force to settle. These involuntary movements of the body, however, result at times into grotesque postures. It is wise to keep an eye on them and check them. For in yoga any involuntary movement of this type is contra. The whole effort in yoga is to raise the level of consciousness, extend the area of its operation; it is retrograde to let unconscious movements creep in.

At times the Force raises up elements that are hidden below the surface in order to expose them to the Light and purify them. The interval between the rise of the disturbing movements and the tangible results of the purifying action, can be trying. The nerves are taut, there is panic in the nervous system and consternation. One needs to be patient and observant during this period. Things do calm down after some time. The same disturbance may be experienced when the Kundalini awakes and starts rising up. Along with it, all kinds of things in the subconscient rise up and throw the system in disorder. Movements of the lower vital and the subterranean physical like hunger, thirst, sex-desire, passions, surge out and create a law and order situation. Of course their momentum slows down as the awakened Force becomes natural and comes under control.

The right attitude for the sadhaka in the face of such disturbances is to refuse to get upset, hold himself in quiet and surrender to the Shakti, whether it acts from above or below.

7-12-'87

64

FEAR

Fear is not natural. Like falsehood, it is an intervention of the Adversary. More than anything else it is the most dangerous element striking at the root of things. It is subtle and for that reason one never knows when it has entered into oneself. It spreads itself all over the being wherever it may have started e.g. in the mind or in the nervous system. However strong one may be, it has an unnerving effect and it weakens the whole structure. Besides, it invites the very thing it is afraid of. Sri Aurobindo puts it vividly:

fear hastening
Towards that of which it has most terror.

Fear has to be nipped in the bud as soon as it enters in the form of a suggestion. It should not be allowed to form itself. One must use one's mental strength to reject it. It is no use to argue and convince the mind that the fear is baseless. There will be counter-arguments and in the process the fear digs itself deep. One must refuse to take cognisance of it. Like most attempts of the hostiles to upset the balance it will not be so easily denied. It persists in coming back. If, however, the strength is exercised without let-up, fear is bound to dwindle away.

One has also to exert one's will to keep out fear from any quarter. Each time there is the cold wind of fear, the will must be asserted to keep it out. By repeated practice, the will-power grows and thoughts of fear do not bother. They may arise or visit suddenly when one does not expect them, but the will which is habituated to throw them out, acts automatically and the coast is kept clear.

And of course there is the spiritual power which the sadhaka learns to develop. He may open to the Power consciously; or it may manifest in him on its own; or he may develop it by judicious use. The spiritual power is indeed the most effective in dealing with the invasions or uprushes of fear. For fear may try to enter from the universal atmosphere or the environment around oneself. Or it may irrupt from the subconscient which may have absorbed suggestions of fear from elsewhere without his being aware of it.

There are different kinds of fear. Fear in the mind, anticipation of unwelcome visitations, may be countered by opposite suggestions. The fear in the vital, however, is more difficult to get rid of. If the vital admits fear, the entire nervous system is affected and half of the normal strength is displaced by an undermining weakness. But fear in the physical is the most obstinate. It acquires a mechanical character and shapes the responses of the body accordingly.

Auto-suggestion may work at a certain level of the mind. Even there it takes a long time to be effective. It does not carry conviction with the physical. A strong

faith in the Power which is summoned and the exposure of the affected part to the Power are required to rectify the situation.
8-12-'87

65

RAKSHASA YOGA

For any one to live absolutely alone is next to impossible. The world is so organised that at every level there is an incessant interchange. In fact this is a law of life adumbrated in the Gita when it speaks of sacrifice, the principle of interchange between men and gods. Even if a person isolates himself physically, he is not alone. There is a constant flow of the world on subtler levels.

In life as it is normally lived, this interaction between persons is an inescapable feature. When two persons get together, there is not only a physical exchange of words or contact through the senses, but also an unseen action between their respective energies. There is a mutual drawing upon each other. If the contact is harmonious they feel happy and want to meet again. If there be some friction, they dislike each other. This interaction mostly takes place on the vital level.

We can see it tangibly in the case of man and woman. There is an interaction of energies, physical or vital, and if the contact is mutually supportive, they are attracted to each other. And this usually develops into what is called love. Each one feels nourished and strengthened by meeting the other and a relation gets established. Even if there is friction in outer life, for whatever reason, they still feel the need of each other. A gap is felt in the absence of this company.

The contact need not always be on the vital or physical level. It may be through thoughts. A person may be physically far away from the other; and yet the latter's thoughts can sail up to him and influence his thinking or feeling. He may not be—and normally he is not—conscious of this influence.

Some persons are by nature expansive. They need to throw themselves out and whether the others like it or not, they squander their apparently inexhaustible energies—mostly vital—on others. The company of such persons is often found invigorating and is sought by others who need some extra supplies. There are also those who are not only expansive but also dominating. They like to stamp their image on others, put their grip on others; they enjoy imposing their possessive hold on people.

There is still another variety of those who do not spend their energies upon others but suck them dry. They are of the nature of vampires who always draw energies from others but never give any to them. Sri Aurobindo cites the instance of husbands whose wives die successively. They do not support their wives but eat them up. Such a situation is known in astrology as *Rākshasa Yoga.*

The ideal state is indeed when both the parties freely participate in the interchange and mutually buttress each other. Normally such a balance is rarely found. But it is possible to make a conscious effort and arrive at a fruitful interchange; this needs good will and willingness to give oneself to the other. Once the will is there, Nature gives a helping hand.

66

INNER STATE

Does conduct build up attitude or attitude shape conduct? Actually it is possible to formulate a code of conduct which need have little to do with a person's true attitude. He may adopt certain ethical rules of conduct and run his life—external life—on those lines. He may be polite and correct in his dealings with others; he may not allow himself to be provoked into rough behaviour. But within he may have a different flow of feeling altogether. His attitude to life may make a distinction between life outside and his own mental formulation.

By and large the attitude of a person influences his reactions to men and things. But this attitude itself is a product of his inner state. Conduct is the outermost part of life. Attitude is something psychological. The inner state is basic—at any rate to the spiritual seeker. He makes a distinction between ethical standards and spiritual principles. The ethical conduct may prepare for spiritual living but it is not the same.

The seeker works to live from within outwards. He forms his attitudes in conformity with his inner state and governs his external conduct accordingly. In other words, he forges a harmony between his inner being, his mental outlook and daily conduct in life. He lays more importance on the inner state than on outer expression. If the inner state is stable and poised in the right consciousness, the outer life tends automatically to express it in conduct.

The governing principle should be spiritual. There

must be enough sincerity in the being to ensure that there is no gulf between the inner and the outer conditions. It is of capital importance in this context to develop a psychic control. The psychic, as we know, never errs. It has a spontaneous discrimination between what is right and what is wrong and its message gets through if the vital and the mind have been trained enough not to interfere. One does not need to weigh the pros and cons according to the ruling ethical codes. What is spiritually right expresses itself through feeling, thought and action. Let us remember that what is spiritual does not conflict with true ethics. Conventional norms of ethical conduct cease to be relevant once the spiritual poise is established.

14-12-'87

67

PSYCHIC CONTROL

Mental control is the first step towards psychic control. What is psychic control and how to set it working?

It is understood that the seeker is awake to the presence of the psychic being in himself. He has become aware that behind the workings of his mind and the movements of his emotional being centred in the heart, there is something deeper which is a concentration of divine consciousness. It is the source of love and harmony, sensitive to all that promotes Godward movement and repellant of what takes away from the good, the right, the truth. The sadhaka develops the habit of looking to it time and again whenever he is confronted with a choice. He learns to feel the psychic vibration and lets it act. Even when he does not need to refer to it, he has a constant remembrance of its presence in himself.

This centration in the psychic is the fulcrum of his organisation of daily life around the Divine. In other words he cultivates the spirit of consecration in his movements and sanctifies all his actions, feelings, thoughts, by offering them to the Divine. This pervading movement of consecration makes it easier for the psychic to extend its influence to the surface and exercise its control over his nature.

This presupposes that he takes steps to build around himself an atmosphere that is favourable to the emergence of the psychic. He is sincere in rejecting whatever may stand in the way of the guidance of the psychic reaching the active intelligence. Mental preferences, vital desires, physical inertia—all these block the psychic functioning on his conscious levels. We do not speak here of interferences from the subconscious layers. They can be detected and thrown out in the measure in which the wakeful parts are responsive to the intimations of the psychic.

When the psychic control is thus established in the being, there is an automatic guidance, from moment to moment. The person does not need to consciously refer to the centre. The psychic which is awake, takes cognisance of all that goes on and sends signals on its own. He has only to act according to the directive, without shilly-shallying on some pretence or other. That way the psychic guidance becomes normalised. Conduct flows spontaneously in the right channels.

15-12-'87

68

IDEA AND EXPERIENCE

There are a number of spiritual truths that are mouthed by many. The Upanishads, for instance, contain a good many formulas, *mahāvākyas* as they are called, enunciating certain fundamental perceptions of moment to man. By repeated utterance, in season and out of season, they have been reduced to cliches. Similarly some of the commandments in the Christian faith. The way men go about, these hardly make any difference in their lives. If these seminal truths are to become effective in life, they must be translated into practice. As Sri Aurobindo puts it, the idea must pass into experience.

Each such idea must be brought down from the mental plane on which it is formulated in words, into life. Its spirit must imbue the being in its becoming. It must form a guideline in shaping attitudes and actual conduct. If there be a divergence in the accepted Idea and the mode of life, the doors are opened to a falsity: insincerity, hypocrisy, deceit, form themselves and vitiate the consciousness. Spiritual integrity demands that there is no gulf between precept and practice. The Idea that ensouls the precept must inform the life-movement at every level: in thought, in feeling, in action. It is only by constant effort to refer each life-situation to the leading Idea that it becomes an experience and the experience stabilises itself in the long run into a realisation.

It is easier and possible to build up a state of being in the light of the Truth-Idea, a passive state forming a background to life. But to render it into active state is more difficult. Sri Aurobindo cites an example: we come across a person who is most brutal in his behaviour. It is naturally difficult to look upon him as divine. How do we meet such a situation? We have to separate the outer man from his inner self and regard the Divine there, possibly suffering the indignity!

It is a matter of sincerity. It takes time, but it is a necessity if we are to be true to ourselves, true to the Idea we cherish. Sincere effort in this direction opens the passage to the psychic which takes over in due course and heals the gulf between the actual and the ideal.

16-12-'87

69

NAME

It was in America. The patient (Indian) in the hospital was still under anaesthesia administered during an operation. The nurse was trying to bring the person back to awareness. She called out the name again and again but there was no response. She had been mispronouncing the Indian name. Someone saw that and had the nurse pronounce the name correctly. Within a few minutes the patient responded and woke up.

Name is something intimate to the person to whom it applies. It is not just a word of appellation chosen indiscriminately. Before a name is chosen for the child, it is common in India to ascertain from the horoscope what are the influences operative in the life just begun, what is the likely nature of the being. And the name is chosen accordingly. Sri Aurobindo and the Mother used to see what was the essential nature of the person, the particular manifestation of consciousness intended in that person, and select an appropriate, significant name.

Even if the name has not been chosen with this significance in view, the being gets used to the given name and responds to it in all conditions. Even in deep sleep, if the name is called, there is a stir somewhere in the being. From this point of view, it is questionable how far the system in vogue (in certain societies) of changing the name of the bride at the time of the marriage, is healthy. The system does undergo a strain in adjusting itself to the altered name which is felt artificial.

From a more serious point of view, the name is an index. Sri Aurobindo speaks of the name as a total of power, qualities and nature of the embodied reality in the form. Each name, so considered, is a power. Properly called, it evokes the concerned reality into action. That is how the Name of God is regarded in the religious or spiritual tradition. Each Name is a mantra. Uttered with concentration and the right attitude, it reaches the Divine Power designated by it and induces its presence in the atmosphere. The Vedic mystics speak of the Name with awe and reverence. They are particular that the enemies in the camp of the Adversary should not come to know of it. It is kept secret, revealed only to the initiated.

No wonder Japa, repetition, of the Name, has played an important part in the quest of man for God. Done with understanding, feeling, identification, it is an unfailing way to contact, link oneself with, to realise the Divine. In some lines of yoga the Name is joined to the breath, to Pranayama, with great effect. In due course the Japa and the Pranayama become automatic and go on all the time even if one is engaged in other activities on the surface. The process becomes natural; the

sadhaka is attentive to it in one of part his consciousness while the rest is occupied otherwise.
17-12-'87

70

THREE TRANSFORMATIONS

Realisation is not transformation. Nor does it necessarily ensure transformation. Realisation is the establishment of an inner spiritual state of consciousness. It is normally the culmination of a series of experiences naturalising the new state in the being. Transformation is the recasting of the entire nature in terms of the realised consciousness. This feature is special to the integral yoga of Sri Aurobindo. In most of the other yogas, the inner realisation has certain inevitable results in the outer nature: there may be some modifications in the mode of reactions, shifts in the ways of reception of contacts etc. But by and large, nature is left to itself—to run its course, as they say. There is no special effort to reach the inner change of consciousness to the functional nature.

This transformation is triple in its kind. First there is the psychic transformation which means the detailed extension of the psychic qualities to the whole of one's nature. Thoughts, emotions, impulses, physical habits—all are subjected to this radical change; they are psychicised. They come to be governed from the psychic centre within. The psychic aroma exudes spontaneously in every detail of life.

This is only the first capital step. Next comes the spiritual. This movement is based on the realisation of the Self that supports everything in manifestation and the infinite Spirit above the mind. This Infinite is realised in its static aspect as well as its dynamic side: its characteristic Peace, Silence, Knowledge, Power, Bliss are opened to and established in the being. Even as this realisation is being built up, there is a sustained effort to communicate these gains to the outer instrumental nature. Their functionings are turned into expressions of the inner spiritual consciousness. Nature is spiritualised. It is also opened to the action of the higher faculties that operate above the thinking mind. Individual nature widens into universal Nature.

The third and culminating movement is the supramental transformation. It means a complete overhauling of the being and nature—at all levels, including the inconscient—so as to become receptacles of the Light of Truth-Consciousness, channels for its Power. Of the three, this is the most difficult operation. For it involves a complete transition from the lower hemisphere, the *trailokyam* of Matter, Life and Mind, to the upper hemisphere of the Gnosis and Sat-Chit-Ananda, from the realm of Ignorance to that of Knowledge. Even when the psychic and the spiritual transformations have gone far, there are obstinate resistances from obscurer regions of nature. It means a replacement of old laws and and processes by new ones. The supramental Power, however, has the capability of overcoming the most rigid obstacle in the Inconscient. When it succeeds in its task there will be hardly any difference between being and nature. They will reveal themselves to be two sides of the same Reality.

18-12-'87

71

DEFECTS AMONG THE REALISED

It is not uncommon to see some of those who are reputed to have realised the Divine behaving in an odd manner. Some hurl abuses at those who go to them with reverence and devotion. Some indulge in disgusting actions in public thoroughfares. There are even some who shock moralists by their sexual propensities. Still one cannot deny that they have attained high states of consciousness within themselves.

The fact of the matter is that there is no coordination between their inner state and outer life. Attention has not been paid to the necessity of bringing the outer nature in line with the consciousness within. Many do not care to do so. They feel that is all part of nature which is best left to itself. They are concerned solely with their inner attunement with the divine consciousness; that is enough for them to attain salvation when the body dies with the exhaustion of its karma. They feel it is a waste of labour to try to reform nature which, in any case, is irrelevant to their central quest.

It is in view of this state of affairs that yogic tradition provides for those who are liberated within but act childlike in life, *bālavat*; those who are inert and shun movement, *jadavat*; those who are incoherent and infrahuman in their tastes, *pishācavat*; those who are violent, unpredictable, *unmattāvat*.

There is another angle to it. Most of these realised beings go beyond the conventional standards of good and evil. Consequently they may not care to conform to the common social norms. They just do what suits

them, their surroundings, their appetites. And they do not think twice about it. Within, they are aloof; in outer life they meet situations as they come without making any fuss about it. You cannot accuse them of lapses from codes which they have beyonded. It is only when they indulge consciously or self-deludedly in unspiritual movements, that you draw the line. And of course they pay the price.
19-12-'87

72

INTERMEDIATE ZONE

Sri Aurobindo draws attention, repeatedly, to the dangers from the inspirations of the vital—the life-world—in sadhana. This is particularly so in the case of persons who are highly imaginative, rajasic by nature and prone to the impulsions of the vital. Indeed there are yogas which make it a point to isolate the vital side and concentrate on the mental or psychic parts. In a yoga like the integral Yoga, however, where action has to take place on all the levels of the being, the danger of the vital allurements is very real.

It all starts with suggestions or voices or visions that flatter the self-importance of the individual. As he turns from the surface preoccupations to his inner levels of consciousness in order to discover his true being at the core of the heart, he finds a large realm of existence opening up. He has to pass through this range of the subtle-physical and the vital energies on his way to the centre. It is here that there is a play of lights and colours, forces of excitement and drive, and the sadhaka is tempted to treat all these as manifestations of the Divine. The voice he hears is likely to be confirmed by subsequent events; that is a strategy to create faith in the authenticity of the voice. It is easy to foresee things from the subtler levels and gain the confidence of the person through premonitary intimations. Or there may be visions that fill him with prospects of glory and if he has any seeds of ambition in him, they are fostered. There may be an inrush of energy making the person feel inordinately strong. In all ways distractions are strewn before him and he tends to luxuriate in those experiences. He avoids corrective agencies, rejects warnings from the soul or the enlightened mind or heart. He imagines he is guided by the Divine; he feels he is an instrument of the Divine; he even goes to the extent—at some stage—of identifying himself with the Divine. In result he misses his true way, he falls a victim to the clever machinations of the Adversary. He gets deluded. The vital power that claims him gives him glittering capacities of impressing others and in no time a gathering forms around him. He becomes a Guru even before he has won his spurs as a disciple.

This misleading zone of vital deceptions is not only between the surface being and the deeper subliminal. It is encountered above the mind when the sadhaka opens the gates of his active mind on the wider expanses above. Apart from the vital part of the mind, there is the vital proper which he has to pass through. Here again, when the Yoga-Shakti works on this plane, there is a throw-up of all sorts of elements that seek to tempt and detain the seeker in their own domain.

Many get lost in this zone which is intermediate between the wakeful surface existence and the deeper or higher regions of spiritual consciousness. The only way to safeguard against these dangers is to ensure adequate purification in the being, opening to the psychic influence and guidance within, trusting to the unfailing Grace of the Divine, directly or through the Guru. Basing all, naturally, there must be a fundamental sincerity. Sincerity, says the Mother, is the safeguard.

20-12-'87

73

FREEDOM

Freedom is fundamental to this manifestation of the Divine. Freedom is the Law. All other laws are only meant to ensure the observance of this basic truth of life. Nature allows full freedom even at the cost of what may appear to the superficial intelligence a dangerous risk. Risk is part of the game and bold spirits take it by the horns.

The Divine allows this freedom even to the Adversary who is intent on destroying this creation. Full freedom is allowed to the play of forces, positive and negative; there is no move to interfere and assert the superior might of the Divine Power and eliminate the hostile elements. There is an intention behind this self-withholding. As Sri Aurobindo observes in *Savitri*, not only the white children but the dark ones also belong to the Divine Mother. The dark ones have chosen a way different from that of their antagonists to participate in the manifestation. They too serve the Divine in an ultimate sense. That is why they are given freedom to work out their propensities and play their unintended role of contributing to the growth of Consciousness by providing a foil to test oneself and increase the strength of will.

It is easy enough for the creative Power to impose blanket restrictions and destroy the offending elements if they do not observe the laws. But that is not the way of the Divine, either as Nature or Supernature. Each is given the liberty to work out his destiny in the manner he chooses. That way alone there is the joy of adventure. It is understood that the freedom of one is not allowed to infringe upon the freedom of another. If it does, life sees to it that a corrective action takes place at some time or other, helping the transgressor to learn his lesson.

Every one has the right to shape his life. He is left free to commit mistakes and learn for himself the consequences thereof. Of course there are those who never learn. It is their prerogative to luxuriate in their wrong paths and pay the price in the long run. From the evolutionary point of view, free growth by experience is more valuable and productive than an imposed conformity in a rule of laws and regulations. What one chooses is more natural; what is foisted by another—individually or collectively—is unnatural and suppressive.

Life becomes interesting, challenging, when there is this freedom of choice. The truth underlying this freedom has the power to ensure growth by learning things by experience. External restrictions narrow the field and limit the growth. The mind should be free to entertain and test for itself ideas and concepts instead of being obliged to subscribe to dogmas and creeds. The heart must have the freedom to choose spontaneously instead of being constricted in the straight jacket of social custom or religious directive. So too the body must have its say in what it wants and what it does not; no set regimen must be prescribed for it. We do not speak here of the vital which appears to need

some scaffolding discipline before it is ready to exercise its legitimate freedom.
21-12-'87

74

ABOUT MEDITATION

It is understood that all do not have to meditate. Each one has his own approach: through devotion, through music, through meaningful study, through dedicated works, through Japa, through Puja—the ways are endless. For those who find meditation helpful in their pursuit of the Divine, it is first essential to note that meditation is not an end in itself; hours of meditation is not relevant for the purpose; it is the quality of meditation that really matters.

For those whose way is through meditation, or at least as an important part of their sadhana, it is important to be regular in their sittings. It will not do to say that we will meditate when the movement is on—a movement of ingathering or descent of peace or an upward pull. Naturally when such moments come, one attends to them, if possible by suspending everything else at that time. What is important is that one must have regular hours or periods for meditation. Whether the mood is on or not, one must make it a point to sit for the session at the fixed time. This regularity creates a habit in one's nature to be receptive at that hour and there is an automatic centration of consciousness; not only in one's own nature but also in the atmosphere around—environing nature. There too a habit forms itself to respond to the call or aspiration. It will be found that something gathers at the fixed hour, waiting as it were for the seeker to receive.

While it is left to each person to choose his own convenient hour—an hour when he is least likely to be disturbed by external calls—there are certain hours that are more helpful than others for this exercise. It is proverbial that the early morning hour—before dawn—is specially fruitful. That is because the active energies in Nature are not yet awake and there is a marked quietude in the air before the movement of activity starts. Similarly the hour of dusk, when the sun sets and energies in Nature begin to draw into quiescence. It is also true that the time of junction between the night and the day, the midnight hour, is highly potent for this purpose. The Jewish tradition prescribes this hour for intense prayer. Similarly the mid-day hour is found to be helpful.

It is not that one must meditate only during these hours—any or all of them. One must be able to go into meditation at any time that one chooses. But to be able to do so, one needs to go through this exercise of regular timings for meditation. This practice leads in some cases to a state when the meditative movement goes on all the time. Regular sittings are not needed at that stage, though one does need to retire into concentrated sessions for special purposes relating to one's own sadhana or to the needs of others.

22-12-'87

75

LIMITATIONS OF THE PHYSICAL

It is not uncommon to hear persons in their sixties saying that they feel as though they were only twenty-five years of age. There is a certain amount of bravado in their posture and what is worse, they proceed to act twenty-five. Naturally not always with happy results! It is not that they make vain boasts. It is their vital body with its flowing energies that feels young. The mind likes to think it is the physical body that is so strong. Very few discriminate between the different parts of their being.

Men think that their energy is a material energy which is increased by physical means. Actually there are physical energies, vital energies, mental energies and even spiritual energies. Each has its own source of supply and sustenance. Normally men are so much identified with their physical body that they tend to attribute all sense of strength, speed, power to the body. Of all the bodies or sheaths, the physical is the most gross and tamasic. It has more limitations than others because it is more rooted in inconscience. Its element of consciousness is decidedly less. That is why it gets tired sooner than the mind or the life-force.

True, the potential of the physical body is great. It has endless reservoir of patience, endurance, resistance. But these potencies are still to be tapped and organised. Till they are developed it is foolhardy to drive the body beyond a reasonable pace. Any kind of excess is bound to evoke reactions of exhaustion, wear and tear, decay in the long run. Long run, because these reactions take time to show. Things slow down, get out of joint, below the surface. They send up signals when the disharmony within goes beyond manageable limits. There are symptoms of illness, minor breakdowns. It is time to look closely into oneself and take steps to rectify.

Respect the body. It is ever at the service of the tyrannical master that is the life-force, the blinkered

governor that is the mind, patiently carrying out their orders as best as it can. It has its own content of consciousness—though not articulate—and its own needs. It is part of this yoga to learn to observe and respond to the call of the body and make it a full-fledged member of one's being. One denies it, starves it, drives it, at one's own peril. If, however, one cultivates the body, tunes oneself to its functionings, it will reveal itself to be superior in some respects to the vital and mental organisations.
23-12-'87

76

CONSEQUENCES OF THE SUPERMIND

There is a good deal of uninformed expectation as well as cynicism at the likely consequences of the descent and establishment of the Supermind. Some think that once the Supermind manifests, all the warring elements in life will disappear as if by magic wand and it will be all milk and honey. There are others who scoff at the prospect of the whole of humanity being divinised.

It is understood that the advent of the Supermind in earth-life will firmly link the lower hemisphere of Matter, Life and Mind with the higher realm of consciousness leading to the Sat-Chit-Ananda. The doors will be opened for the direct action of the powers of the intuitive and overmental worlds. There is bound to be a fillip to the forces of harmony and unity. The hard resistance of the Inconscient is sure to start yielding. And there are many more changes to follow.

But this does not mean that all humanity will be transformed. Only those who are prepared and open to the action of the new principle will be the receptacles of the new Consciousness. The rest will have only indirect benefits: the general level of living will be elevated to a higher status; the operations of the mind will undergo changes, they will be more open to the light and knowledge of Truth.

When Sri Aurobindo was asked if suffering would disappear, he replied that suffering is a result of Ignorance. As long as one remains under the rule of Ignorance, pain and suffering are inevitable. Ignorance leads to division. Division promotes separativity. The underlying sense of oneness is lost, with the result that every impact comes from the 'other' with its reactions depending upon the ability of the person to harmonise with it. The advent of the Supermind which is a power of Unity will surely work to restore the hidden truth of oneness into action. But it will operate directly only among those who are eligible to participate in the rule of the gnostic consciousness.

The coming of the Mind in this creation has not abolished the orders of existence which are infra-mental. They continue as gradations of the evolving spirit. So too the existing humanity will largely continue with a new rung added to it. The initial change will be in a few. From them it has to spread out, making others ready for a similar change. No miraculous transformation can be expected.

24-12-'87

77

GURU

Speaking of Gurus, there is often a comparison between one Guru and another. There are discussions of who is greater than others. It is largely a clash of conviction with conviction. Truth to tell, among those who are qualified to be Gurus there should be no comparisons. For each has his own line of realisation, each has his position in the manifestation of the Divine Consciousness. Each goes to the limit of his destined achievement. The realisation of one does not invalidate the realisation of another. Both are true in their respective settings. Each is suited to a corresponding disposition. It is a question of affinity, the direction that is natural to the seeker.

Consequently the seeker must find out what exactly is his objective in approaching the Reality. Instead of trying to assess the relative merits and grades of the Gurus, he must ascertain his own position. And if he is sincere in his quest, he is led to the Guru who is appropriate to his needs. If he has to search, his choice falls upon one who is relevant to his inner necessity. How to be sure that one's choice is the right one? This is a frequently asked question.

Usually one recognises the Guru meant for oneself by instinct. There is no reasoning process involved in the choice. When one is in the presence of such a Guru, one has an inner sense of arriving. One feels at home. There is a deep peace and felicity. There is mutual recognition. Subsequent happenings reveal that the meeting has not been an accident but the working of a Design. Everything has led to it.

If, however, there is excitement, a kind of intoxication in the encounter, one needs to wait before rushing to conclusions. More often it is a vital impact and the seeker is likely to float in that energy. It is his surface being that is thus exposed and undergoes the expanding experience; the soul within is not touched, on the other hand it is more likely to get veiled. When the Guru is the right one, the contact quietens the vital and draws forward the inner being.

There is another angle to the question. There is an authentic spiritual tradition that even if the 'Guru' is not what one takes him to be, if one has deep faith in him, the Divine sees to it that he does not come to grief. It is a question of sincerity in the aspiration. It is a sage counsel that instead of worrying about the credentials of the Guru, the seeker must work on himself and prepare to be the proper disciple. He must strive to become a worthy disciple. When he does that he will find the Guru waiting for him.

25-12-'87

78

'I'

Man's life revolves round his 'I'. He imagines he is a self-sufficient person running his own life. He has a mind that thinks what he wishes to, a will that executes what he wants. But is he really free? Has he the freedom to think and act as he chooses? Is his personality something that is independent of the world and does he really have an effective initiative?

If we look closer into his constitution we find that he rarely acts on his own. Most of his life is spent in responding to contacts from outside. In fact his body itself is a kind of vibratory mechanism that responds to impacts and situations all the time. Besides what is he himself? He comes to birth with a load of karma: the energies that he released in the past births have accumulated and are pressing for expression. They shape, largely, his temperament, his volitions, his attitudes. Then he has his share of heredity. He carries in himself the characteristic elements of the nature of his parents—even ancestors—which insist upon fulfilling themselves. Added to it, there is the sum of what he gathers in his present life. All together they form a formidable combination severely limiting his freedom of action. All of it comes to life under favourable conditions which are provided by Nature. The whole operation is woven around the sense of 'I'—the ego-formation which itself is constituted by Nature. And this 'I' turns out to be a very fragile entity ever exposed to invasions from the larger life around. Where, then, is the freedom for man?

There is. The freedom is there deep within in the purusha who is the bedrock of individual existence. At the core of the being there is the Person, an individualised formation of the Spirit as the Divine Purusha at the head of this manifestation. He is the central self which is eternal and infinite in its consciousness. It is not a formation of Nature, not a product of extraneous elements like heredity, karma etc. This Person puts forward many personalities in the movement of evolution. Even within the individual existence, the central purusha is projected or reflected on each level of nature as the corresponding purusha. Thus we have the *annamaya purusha*, physical being, *pranamaya purusha*, life being, *manomaya purusha*, mental being and so on. These purushas again have two statuses: the outer personality identified with the surface nature and the inner being which embodies the consciousness of the central purusha more closely. Man is free to the extent he lives in the consciousness of this individual purusha which is organised for individual expression in the purushas presiding over their respective levels of nature.

This individual purusha-entity, Sri Aurobindo points out, is always conscious of its identity with the Cosmic Purusha. It can open out into the cosmic dimension of existence when it chooses. It is of course understood that man has to grow aware of this inmost entity and become one with it before he can have the cosmic liberation.
26-12-'87

79

COSMIC LIBERATION

Liberation into the cosmic consciousness takes place when the individual breaks out of his separativity. Normally he is shut up within the walls erected by his ego and feels and acts in division from others. He lives apart, in his consciousness, from others and from the world at large. He forgets totally the underlying oneness between himself and the rest. This unity is in fact anterior to his experience of separation; it is never, really, lost. It is only covered up by the divisive movements of his surface nature which is subject to the prevailing Ignorance. It is possible to get back to the basic unity by yogic means; occasionally it happens all of a sudden without any special effort on one's part. That is a kind of culmination of a movement that has been gathering, perhaps in a previous birth. Or it can be an act of Grace; in either case the being has got to be ready for the experience.

The individual no longer feels a distinct person as one normally does. He realises his identity with the Self that is one in all; he is delivered by the finite into the Infinite; he discovers in himself a status that is immobile, unchanging, unacting; the usual dualities of life cease to have meaning for him. At the level of this Self where he finds himself stationed, there is an overpowering experience of oneness of All. This is the static aspect of the realisation. It is possible to rest in it, content with it. But there is also another aspect: the dynamic.

In this experience the individual realises his status of participation in the Becoming of the Cosmic Being. The precise nature of his realisation depends upon where the opening takes place. If it is the mind, he becomes one with the cosmic mind; if it is on the vital plane, he feels his unity with the cosmic vital; if on the physical, the body feels its oneness with the universal Matter.

This opening need not be only horizontal. It can be vertical too. In the course of the yogic effort, one exerts pressure of ascension on the barrier or the lid above the mind; or one invokes the higher Power to act on the lid. And when this enclosing wall (or lid) is broken, the individual consciousness joins the Infinite, feels one with it or feels as though it is the Infinite. And it gets into tune with the larger, the cosmic Consciousness in its Power aspect. Whichever the plane of his being on which this identity is realised, he feels himself a centre or a channel for the universal action on that level. His personal identity becomes, so to say, a fiction. 27-12-'87

80

EMPTINESS

Men are so used to the constant running of thoughts that if there be any slowing of the activity or even a seeming arrest, they get alarmed. They complain that their mind is going blank and they rush back to the normal hectic movement. Intellectuals like Russell have complained of it; even practitioners of yoga have got alarmed that they are on the verge of madness. Actually thought-activity is not the original nature of the mind. It is more a habit of nature than an inherent character. The mind is meant to be a quiet reflector of knowledge, of ideas from above its level. The run of thoughts in the average mind prevents this function. That is why in any deep culture of the mind or in yoga, the first step is to gain control over the mental activity, restore some order in its normal chaos, regulate its thought-movements. The aim is to silence the mind, keep it in a state of receptivity to higher influxes. In other words to empty the mind of its mechanical thoughts. After a serious effort the sadhaka arrives at such a state, at least during his periods of meditation or concentration.

Sri Aurobindo speaks of three kinds of emptiness. The first one is not really empty; it is full of the Divine Presence. It is only empty of thoughts. One feels full with what accompanies the Presence: a peace, or power or a sense of clarity or whatever. The second type is something neutral. It originates no thoughts. But if they come in from outside, it watches them without getting involved in them or reacting to their positive or negative character. It stays unmoved. Some may feel a dryness about it. They may miss the *rasa* element in the mental attitudes. Others may experience a dullness, disinclination to move—mentally or emotionally—and complain about it. That happens at times with this neutral state of emptiness. But with vigilance this tendency can be kept down and rejected. The third kind is the result of a relentless yogic operation: throwing out of thoughts with a will and at the same time not letting thoughts from outside come in. This may be described as creating a vacant mind which is still, alert, waiting for some higher charges to fill it. It is a strenuous exercise but those with a strong will and power of concentration do succeed in it after a patient effort. Indeed it is possible that this vacancy or emptiness in the mind may be the result of a strong spiritual impact, say from a God-realised person or one who has himself achieved this *siddhi*. Or it can be a sheer Grace.

Emptiness of mind is always an excellent condition for the Divine Consciousness to act. Of course there is the danger of wrong forces taking advantage of the situation where mental discrimination is kept suspended. But if one has, side by side, cultivated the psychic contact, then the psychic discrimination can be depended upon to avert such dangers.
1-4-'88

81

ASURIC TAPASYA

The Purunas are full of legends describing the terrific austerities undergone by men of yore. Of course not all of them were for spiritual purposes. Some set about with the specific aim of acquiring occult powers, extraordinary powers. And there have been quite a few who did things ostentatiously to impress the gullible and gain popularity.

These practices are not so widely done these days. But the attraction of hard austerity is still there. It may lie in denying the body its normal, legitimate needs. Some reduce the quantity of food to the minimum; some go on long fasts; some minimise the hours of sleep.

There is another category of those who sit tight on their sense-faculties. Some seal their lips, some put bands over their eyes. Some would not so much as look at women. This kind of forcible self-denial, unnatural suppression has been unambiguously condemned in the Gita as hurting the Indweller.

It is not that they are totally without value. Kept within healthy limits, these practices help in acquiring control over the physical body, its functionings, the vital and its impulses. They draw out the potential of the body and the life-energy and enlarge the field of self-effectuation. But they have no spiritual value as such. On the other hand, such feats of strength, endurance and mastery over one's material and vital nature, tend to blow up the ego. There is no change in the consciousness of the person. The adept is self-satisfied in the crudity of his nature.

A certain element of external discipline is indeed essential in any line of spiritual life. It is necessary to ensure adequate health of the body and smooth operations of the pranic energy. A selection of asanas and pranayama exercises should help in preparing the base, the *ādhāra*. Patanjali states categorically that these form the externals of the yoga-discipline. But to overdo them, exaggerate their role is almost pointless in the spiritual context. They develop into fads, fetishes if they are innocent. But if designed to impress the laity, to make a pompous display of one's physical or vital siddhis, they turn into traps. They distract from the main purpose, they deflect.

2-4-'88

82

REALISATIONS

There is not one type of spiritual realisation. The Divine yields itself to be realised in many ways. Each travels by the route for which he is temperamentally suited. It is indeed very important to know which is one's way. Mere attraction or any kind of imposition does not work in the long run. Usually it is the Guru who guides in these matters, though on rare occasions the Divine shows the way directly in an unmistakable manner.

There is the way which is time-tested, the realisation of the Self. There is the basic reality within oneself, unchanging, immutable, eternal. It is the Self which stands behind all the shifting movements and personalities across births and deaths. At some point in one's life, there is an awakening to the existence of this Self, Atman, and a compulsive necessity to realise the truth of this Self. One takes steps to gradually disentangle oneself from involvements in the movements of external nature and turns the gaze inward. Indeed there are conditions like detachment, purification, intensity of aspiration, Grace, which are to be fulfilled before the destination is reached: Self-realisation.

There is another way to the Divine, approach through a chosen Form which serves as a symbol, *pratika*. It may be the Form of a Deity with human features or a linear representation like the Mandala. The Form is chosen as a channel of communication. It becomes a focus for the seeker's aspiration, adoration and identification. In the measure of his faith and active communion through prayer, Mantra, surrender etc. the Presence makes itself felt in the chosen centre and an eventual fusion of the human and the divine consciousness takes place. There are traditions which do not accept that there can be union between the human and the Divine; they envisage a close proximity and intimate relationship between the two.

Yet another way is to learn to expand and deepen one's gaze on the world. Breaking through the surface appearances one becomes aware of the divine Presence, a pervasion by the Divine Being—Brahman as they term it in the Upanishads. This opens the door to the realisation of the cosmic or universal Divine. Gradually one's consciousness expands and gets identified with the cosmic consciousness which is based on Oneness of all creation, a Unit of All.

And there are so many other ways. In all of them there is a strong effort on the part of the individual to change the mundane character of his normal living into an increasingly spiritual existence till he realises the Divine Reality. They are Divine realisations.

Distinct from these is what Sri Aurobindo calls the Divine's realisation. Here it is the Divine, the Self, that plays the dominant role. The individual is receptive and lets the Divine work in himself. Of course he does an enabling sadhana; to control and conquer his lower nature with the aid of the higher Power. The Divine chooses to reveal itself in him, the Self bares its body—to use the language of the Katha Upanishad. Here it is the Divine that is truly the sadhaka, the sadhana and the siddhi.

83

DEFECTS IN YOGIS

Most men tend to be charitable to themselves: they explain away to their own satisfaction their wrong movements and actions. They even wonder why they are not appreciated sufficiently enough. But when it concerns others, they are severe in their judgment. Especially in the case of those who are great by all accounts, they are quick to detect the smallest deviation from accepted norms and lose their sense of proportion.

This may be seen more prominently in the case of yogis or those who are revered as Gurus. The disciples forget their own failings but affect to be shocked by 'unspiritual' movements in those who are in any case more advanced than themselves. This is a very wrong perspective in which the fault-finders are the losers.

These yogis have admittedly attained some higher states of consciousness. They have practised disciplines, observed the required conditions, and have grown in stature. Each such person adding to the common stature, exceeding the normal humanity in any direction, is a gain to mankind. Sri Aurobindo asks us to look to this aspect of things. Look to the achievement in the person, to the positive features of his attainment. That way you too will grow in that mould.

If on the other hand men devote undue attention to negative elements in the person, they stand to lose. Their reservations, their doubts, cut across whatever communication is opened up between them and the Guru or yogi. Even an Avatar carries with himself the load of *samskāras* of the family, the society in which he is born and reared. They do colour his life in some way. We cannot judge him from our standards of a different age. We forget that an Avatar too is in a human body and shares human imperfections, at least in his surface being. Similarly the yogin has a part of himself which is a product of his environment; the type of life that he had to lead in his pre-yogic days does leave some marks on his personality and nature. It will not do to exaggerate these elements forgetting the much that is outstanding on the positive side. Some yogis have queer habits which are clearly a legacy of the past. Some have an understandable vanity, some like to drop names with obvious intentions. But all such features are clearly of minor importance. In the overall setting of the spiritual stature of the person they should be ignored and left out of our gaze. Actually some yogis are more loved for their foibles which bring them nearer the common folk. And some of them know it.

7-4-'88

84

NOT TO ASK FOR THINGS

There are some disciplines which advise a rule of life by which the sadhaka undertakes not to ask for things from anybody. It is understood that the observance of this rule is backed up by a corresponding attitude in the being. Even a mental pressure is avoided. The idea seems to be to exercise a control over desire with a view to eliminating it totally.

Those who practise this discipline keep a strong faith that what they truly need will come to them by a divine dispensation. What is not forthcoming is not needed. They have this faith in the Divine and their acceptance of the divine Will is complete. This involves, necessarily, a complete surrender to the Divine in the trust that the Divine does what is needed at every moment—at any rate for those who leave things to its Will.

Sri Aurobindo cites one or two cases of such persons who had the responsibility of looking after collectivities. They never thought of the morrow. The Mother had this approach, not as a discipline but as an attitude to life which came naturally to her following her total submission to the Will of the Supreme Divine. She was always calm and unworried even when the finances of the Ashram seemed precarious. She did not even approve of the disciples asking others for money. It was her conviction that if one had the right attitude of trust and surrender, what was really needed would be made available. It is evident this is not just a question of mental acceptance. It should be backed up by the vital without a tremor of expectation or frustration. It is a capital step in sadhana when this practice becomes natural.

85

ILLNESSES IN YOGA

For an earnest sadhaka of the integral yoga every experience has a meaning. Every incident has some significance. Nothing happens without some message. He learns to be vigilant and to look deeper for the why and how of the happening. Nothing is insignificant to him, everything in God's manifestation has a purpose.

Even ostensibly casual circumstances have some relation to his inner situation. He is conscious of this fact in the life of every one who dedicates his life to the Divine.

In this setting even illnesses have a meaning. Apparently they may be due to some viruses in the air, contagion in the environment. Still if they can find entry into the atmosphere of one who is protected by a higher Power, there must be some door that is open at some level of the being. The yogi treats no malady as casual. Even if it is a common cold, he looks into himself, looks around, and spots the precise contact that has given rise to this reaction. For him, every illness has a psychological reason behind it. He probes into his life-movements, thought-currents, emotional changes even as he looks into possible resistances in his physical body, to find out the hidden causes of the disorder. He also learns to spot any failures of attitude at his spiritual level. In other words he finds out the cause of the illness within himself and takes steps to correct the disequilibrium.

It is when the sadhaka takes each physical sickness as an occasion to scrutinise his movements behind the surface levels and works to set right the direction of his life that we can say that even illnesses become occasions for progress in yoga. Commonly men tend to blame outer conditions when any illness makes appearance. Of course we do not take into account here upsets due to obvious physical causes like indigestion, wrong exposure etc. though even there, if the nervous envelope is strong these attacks are automatically thrown off. In yogic life, for instance, it is considered important to be careful of one's contacts with people of all sorts. But things are not always under one's control. In a collective life, particularly, contacts are unavoidable however undesirable they may seem. A yogi who has learnt his lesson, does not blame any external provocation for his state of health. He looks into himself and finds out where he is weak in his nervous being and how the contact has touched that subnormal spot. The Mother observes that one can pass through a plague area and yet be untouched provided one has taken the necessary steps to fortify one's faith in the protection of the Divine and close chinks in the nervous being.

86

PROBLEM OF EGO

The ego is admittedly a formidable challenge that every seeker has to face in spiritual life. It is possible, to a great extent, to exercise control over the ego and abstain from actions or words that are egoistic. Ethics, morality, precepts of religion, are all there to curb unseemly movements of the ego that offend the social sense of decency. At best, as a result of such sustained efforts to tailor one's behaviour in life, egoism can be put under the carpet. But the ego remains, in however subtle a manner.

The standard way to deal with the ego in spiritual discipline is to raise the consciousness above the mental level and expand its horizons so that one comes under the influence of the universal Self, the Atman. Gradually the seeker identifies himself with this Self and realises the same Self in all. When he realises his identity with the cosmic Divine the mental sense of ego dwindles. The mind gets freed from the compulsive action of the ego.

But the vital nature is not touched on that account. It retains its ego-character and is obstinate in its refusal to give up its ego-motivation. At this juncture it is the psychic opening that proves of great help. The humility that ensues with the growing influence of the psychic acts as a corrective and the ego recedes. Thus the realisation of the Spirit above the mind is seconded by the realisation of the psychic at the centre of the being and this joint action dissolves much of the ego.

Though the mental and the vital ego are put behind, there is still the ego in the physical and the subconscient. But they are not so obtrusive and they can be left to the care of the Yoga-Force to which the sadhaka opens himself.

It is understood that humility which plays a key role in the elimination of the vital ego is not an outward humility. It is a pervading sense and active feeling that there is one Spirit everywhere, an ocean as it were of which one is merely a wave. When one realises the immensity of the Self and the innate nature of the Consciousness as Love, there is a spontaneous surge of humility in the heart and the aggressive ego slinks away. Thus both the spiritual and the psychic realisations join in destabilising the ego.

87

THE PSYCHIC NOT ENOUGH

It is often asked if realisation of the psychic being is not enough as a spiritual goal. Why is it necessary to realise the Spirit, the Divine in the universe? If the objective is to attain union with the inner Divine, then indeed realisation of the psychic should be adequate. It is an individual achievement and goes no farther. If however, it is sought to extend the realisation to other parts of the being, particularly as related to the universe, then that is not enough. For the psychic is individual in character. One who is in union with it feels himself as one in the many but not as one with the many. For that purpose he needs to realise the Spirit on his higher mental levels. The mind is disciplined to open to the universal Self and identify itself with it. One who realises this Self realises also the Divine Reality as manifest in the universe. The Divine 'I' replaces the individual 'I'.

The psychic may throw its influence on the rest of the being but by and large, the individual nature is left to function on its own steam. The psychic needs the individual for its functioning. That is not so with the spiritual Self: The Divine 'I' does not need to function on the basis of individual nature. The universal nature forms the needed instrumentation. In other words the emphasis shifts from the personal to the impersonal.

Strictly speaking, one who realises his identity with the cosmic Self on his higher mental levels and beyond, does not need to bring in the psychic in his scheme of things. It is only if he wants to transform his individual being that it becomes necessary to turn his attention to the psychic being and establish its governance. The working of the psychic has a powerful purificatory effect on the rest of the being and that makes it easier to control and transform the vital nature and change the allegiance of the vital being.

It may be added that the two realisations are not two compartmentalised movements. Each can help the other. Spiritualisation does exert pressure on the being and the founts of the psychic open up and flow out. Similarly when the psychic casts its influence on the mental being, it loses its rigidity and fans out into the larger extension of the Spirit. It is certainly possible, as in the integral yoga, to work upon both simultaneously —in the heart and in the mind. At some stage one comes to realise that both the Self and the psychic are the same Reality in different functional poises.

88

DOCTOR OR MEDICINE?

It is a fairly common experience that the same medicine does not always work even though the illness is the same. At times one reads the advertisements and goes in for particular drugs but there is no guarantee that they will act.

The same medicine effects differently when prescribed by different doctors. This raises the question whether medicines have an intrinsic power to cure or it is the doctor who really matters. Experience confirms that it is the personality of the doctor that plays the major role. Some doctors have the gift of healing power. This power may exude through their hands or their personality. The moment such a doctor comes into one's atmosphere, one starts feeling better. Sri Aurobindo observes that medicines lend their properties to such a power of the physician.

Usually some persons carry this healing power in their nature. It is not something taught or cultivated. It is a born gift. More people have this capacity in themselves than normally supposed. A successful healer once pointed out that men are not usually aware of this power in their hands. They wake up to it at some point, by accident or by happy revelation. Of course it needs to be tended. The moment one becomes aware of this capacity, one takes steps to develop it by practice, by close attention. At times it may happen that the power may be communicated by an adept.

It is understood that this healing power is something impersonal. It is a universal force that acts through a fit channel. The art of healing is to let the Power get through. Some doctors do it more easily than others. They have the apt temperament and capacity to get into the atmosphere of the patient through a kind of identification. An easy bridge is established between the physician and the patient and the healing power works without any block. The confidence created by the doctor ensures a quicker action. Medicines are more or less a make-believe in common cases. Even when they are specially called for, they act through the power of the physician.

89

SPIRITUAL MOVEMENTS AND FAILURE

It is a common question: Why do most spiritual movements that start with great promise tend to fade out sooner or later, leaving the distraught world as it was? So many Saviours have come and gone, but things remain what they have always been. Some go on to argue that all spiritual programmes are impractical and end in disillusionment.

A closer analysis of the phenomenon, however, reveals a distinct pattern which does not justify such pessimism. In the present organisation of the world which is under the rule of Ignorance and its brood of limitations, darkness and its ultimate result—Falsehood —any attempt at an establishment of Truth meets with opposition. And that is understandable. The Powers of Negation that rule the earth will not oblige by yielding any of their fief without struggle. They want to retain their kingdom and resist with all their might every effort to displace them by the affirmative Powers of Truth, Light, Peace. They try all means at their disposal: misrepresentation, disinformation, persecution, assault.

This does not always succeed, at any rate, fully. The inherent Right and Truth of the movement withstands the opposition and gains ground in the first flush of its impact on the world. When obstruction and open opposition do not succeed in their objective, the Adversary changes his strategy. The negative elements mix themselves up with the main stream of the movement. They enter in order to work and wreck from within. They dilute the purity of the organisation by sowing doubts in the minds of the faithful, diverting the energies into wrong channels—of course under specious names—and in all ways creating a defeatist atmosphere. In politics we call this dissidence; in spiritual contexts they function as outposts of the Enemy. Indeed, all may or may not be conscious of the role they are made to play.

Sri Aurobindo is reported to have once observed that among his disciples were some anti-divine elements who had come for transformation. He was charitable. When the Mother was asked why certain persons who should never have been in the Ashram—on any of the spiritual standards—were active in the collectivity, she replied that they had been attracted by the Power of the place. Whatever the ostensible reason or reasons, the fact remains that spiritual movements have always got to be on guard against vital mixtures which vitiate from within and strive to utilise the strength of the higher thrust for their own ends.

We may note in passing that this feature may be observed not only in spiritual matters but equally in other fields of life where positive efforts are made for change of the existing, unsatisfactory order.

Purity must be maintained at any cost. There can be no real failure where sincerity and purity are kept up.
15-4-'88

90

"AUROBINDOISM"

There are some words whose current usage has wandered far from their original meaning. It is not that literal meaning no longer holds good. The acquired connotation preponderates. In Sanskrit they make a distinction between the direct meaning of a word and its indirect meaning. It is called *lakshanā*, indication. Very often it is the latter that conveys the intention of the author. One such term is 'ism'. Originally it may have meant a doctrine or principle of a person or a philosophy. But today it has a sense of limitation, limitation to the view held with an implied rejection of what does not cohere with it. Doctrine degenerates into dogma.

Years ago a professor of philosophy in the Calcutta University used the word, "Aurobindoism". Sri Aurobindo confesses to a sense of shock on reading it.

And that is natural. For as the Mother points out, Sri Aurobindo's formulation of his Knowledge is not a teaching, not even a revelation but a decisive action direct from the Supreme. In other words it is continuous unfoldment of a Truth that is seeking to manifest itself. It is not something that can be neatly folded and bound within the covers of a book. It is not a formula or set of formulas erected by him for others to conform to. It is not a well-tailored suit for his followers to wear. It is a Vision and an approach, based upon it, to the future of the Earth-life. It is as broad as the universe and permits no stratification. It is as supple as life itself. It can be and is practised in a hundred ways. There is no 'ism' about it.

I have always had a shrinking feeling whenever I come across usages like 'Aurobindoism', 'Aurobindonian', 'Aurobindoite' etc. These terms carry a certain negative imputation. They limit the truth for which Sri Aurobindo stands. His is no religion, no cult, no sect, no regimented group. His is a universal message, It is difficult to find another mind with such a catholic, comprehensive outlook. The sweep of his consciousness excludes nothing. His cosmic vision finds the justification for every stand, every movement. A true follower of Sri Aurobindo is necessarily a universal man in the making. You cannot put a label on him as belonging to a particular group, isolating him from the rest of his fellow-beings. While he bases his life on some large, verifiable, truths of Nature (and Supernature), he is not blind to the need of other possible approaches for others who are in a different line of evolution. In his consciousness he embraces the world. It is truly an offence against the universality of Sri Aurobindo to reduce the meaning of his life to an 'ism' or categorise those who practise

his message of Life Divine and seek to live it for the benefit of the world, as particular 'ians' or 'ites'.
16-4-'88

91

SAINTS AND SAGES

It is easy enough to recognise a saint. He is one who has realised oneness with his *antarātman*, the psychic being, and is ever in union with this Divine Entity within. He exudes the inalienable qualities and powers of the psychic: warmth, happiness, joy, love. Wherever he lives or goes, these radiations spread round and impact on the environment. He is a Bhakta, surrendered in devotion to the Lord. He sees the Lord everywhere, in everyone. To him all is God. He does not, in fact cannot, hate anybody. We may say he has realised the Divine in his heart.

A spiritual person who has realised his objective, comes under a different category. He has a consciousness that is spiritual in character. It is not subject to the rule of ignorant nature. He lives normally above the mind as we know it. His vision is broader, higher. Unlike the saint whose realisation is individual, he becomes universal in his consciousness. He is open to a knowledge that is based on Truth; his means of knowledge are not those of the intellect but more intuitive or revelatory. The range of his wisdom is more comprehensive. He is a Sage who sees beyond the immediate.

In other words, his attainments are in the realm of consciousness with knowledge, vision, power, playing their dominant role. His being is one with the Divine, whether in its personal or impersonal aspect. We may say, his is a realisation more impersonal than personal. This is not to say that there cannot be both. In fact an integral realisation with the personal and the impersonal as its two wings is not only possible but a desideratum in a total approach.

A spiritual man need not be a saint. He may not choose to realise the Divine in his heart centre and manifest the Love aspect. His nature may incline him towards the Knowledge aspect. He may prefer to spread out and identify himself with the cosmic manifestation of the Divine, thus realising the universality of the Truth in manifestation. He may not have the external appearance that is associated with holiness in the popular mind. His external life-modes may not conform to conventional standards. But that does not make any difference to the state of his consciousness which is one with the Divine.

The saint and the sage are in fact two grades in the evolution of the Spirit. They both point to the next stage in this evolution, the advent of the Gnostic Being who is both the saint and the sage in being and becoming.
18-4-'88

92

YOGIS AND PHILOSOPHERS

Each yogi, worth the name, has an experience. Either he has worked for it or it has come to him and he has followed it up by way of stabilisation. So far so good. If he has the capacity, he can communicate that experience and a following forms of those who learn from him or those who admire him for his achievement. But not all the yogis stop with the organisation of their experience. They try to build a philosophy. They seek to explain everything on the basis of their experience. This often fails to stand the scrutiny. In the process the experience itself becomes suspect.

Philosophy, especially a spiritual philosophy, indeed needs to base itself on experience. But it has other ramifications too. It seeks to relate experience to the Reality which goes beyond a single experience or viewpoint. It attempts to explain the principles and processes of life—physical, vital, mental and spiritual. It is only a large mind, a supple intellect helped by a certain intuitive insight that can formulate a valid philosophy.

Like the yogi who tends to limit himself in his experience, the philosopher too swears by his own perceptions. Both are found to deny the validity of other possible experiences and philosophies. They forget that life is larger than logic, that the Infinite cannot be exhausted by a single experience or series of experiences in the same line; it cannot be contained in any one formulation. The philosopher should know that the Reality admits several approaches to it and its many aspects lend themselves to different formulations. Similarly the yogi must admit there are other possible experiences which cast a different light on the Reality.

To be able to extend one's vision and look constructively at other realisations, other standpoints, requires a catholicity of mind, a readiness to extend the boundaries of one's finitude. A true philosophy is one which is able to see and appreciate the starting points of other systems, the place they occupy in the total situation of the unveiling of the many-sided Reality; it is also concerned with integrating them in the scheme of the spiritual evolution of consciousness. A true yogi is he

who recognises that that the Reality yields itself to be realised by each one in the mould of his nature and line of soul-evolution; he does not rush to fit in the universe in the frame of his single experience.
20-4-'88

93

FREEDOM IN ACTIVITY

The Gita asks for disinterested action. It is a call for activity without personal motivation. To do this with any measure of success the doer must get rid of his ego. And that is not easy. There are many egos, each hiding behind the other. It is only a change in consciousness that can ensure action that does not create karma, does not bind.

Sri Aurobindo speaks of three ways in which this can be done: to be free in consciousness. The first is to learn to separate the Purusha from the Prakriti. In each detail one must observe oneself and stand aloof from the Prakriti; the Purusha must not get involved, get lost in the movement of Prakriti. This discipline gradually leads to settling oneself in the Witness status. It may be said that even in the act of witnessing—and impliedly sanctioning—there is an element of karma. But that is minimal.

The second way is to realise the Self, Atman, that is not identified with the universe; it is independent of Nature. By sadhana it is possible to realise its presence and station oneself in it. The cosmic movement does not affect the being. It is not even a witness. One stays identified with the Self that does not concern itself with the universal movement.

The third way is to attain union with the Transcendent Reality. By realising the Paramatman which exceeds and is above the action of universal Nature, one is in no way affected by the activity that is inevitable in life in the world.

Allied to this position is the way to lose oneself in the Void described by the Buddhists. One dissolves the various elements of nature and what is left of the person is merged in the 'Nothing' that is the ultimate of everything, in that approach. Whether it is at all possible for the soul to thus lose its identity in a Void is debatable. All the same, in yoga, it is helpful to experience this state of void in which the world is felt to be unsubstantial. One gets out of the world as a formation of Ignorance. The false appearance must go before the true nature of the world can reveal itself.

These are positive ways in which one does not have to fight with the ego that is the lynch-pin of all bondage. The ego thins out and dies by itself as these spiritual states establish themselves in one's consciousness.
22-4-'88

94

SPIRITUAL COMMUNITIES

Spiritual collectivities represent the aspiration in mankind to form and live a life of the spirit. By and large they are an effort to grow beyond the limitations of the common human life—physical, vital, mental—and imbibe a higher and freer consciousness. The goal is a liberation from the hold of lower nature into the freedom of the Self. In certain lines of discipline, like the Buddhist, it may be a self-dissolution in Nirvana. Whatever the precise nature of the goal, the communities are organised around a spiritual ideal. They may pursue different disciplines corresponding to their aims.

The quality of the life in these movements depends upon the quality of the consciousness lived by the individuals. The key is the individual. The more the number of individuals who practise these higher values the more spiritual is the character of the collectivity. Naturally one cannot wait till the full realisation is attained. It is enough if there is spiritual experience, an experience that inspires and moves at least some of the members. It is understood that all are not siddhas; all are sadhakas, practitioners of the sadhana.

Here again it is inevitable there are varying levels of consciousness in the collective life. Sri Aurobindo points out in *The Life Divine*, how in such a collectivity of seekers, the difficulties in nature of each may stand out more prominently than elsewhere. In the special atmosphere where there is a constant pressure for exceeding one's nature, the reactions are bound to be sharp. There is no such urgent pressure in ordinary life and one can get along with all one's imperfections in a world that is admittedly imperfect.

There is another feature that is commonly seen in the history of spiritual communities. They flourish in their line, show an amazing vitality and capacity for growth, when the Founder is alive. Usually he is one who has realised the truth of the Ideal that is pursued and he wields the Power of that consciousness with striking effect. Things naturally go on splendidly as long as he is there or at any rate as long as he keeps up the purity and intensity of his realisation for the benefit of others. The situation begins to change when he is no longer fully effective or he passes away. Thereafter the usual and natural movement of decline sets in. But that need not be always so. If the consciousness of the leader has been imbibed and kept living among the disciples—at least a few of them—then the movement can continue with almost the same dynamis. What is important is that the fundamentals of the sadhana must have been assimilated and organised in the lives of these disciples, in the life-time of the Teacher. Other flames should be already burning. More lamps come to be lit in the very order of nature.

The life and future of each community is determined by the sincerity and inner commitment of a core of sadhakas totally dedicated to the Ideal. External circumstances and features play a secondary, almost a minor role.

23-4-'88

95

LIFE AS TEACHER

The mind is a divisive faculty. It always functions by selecting its areas of operation and concentrating upon them to the exclusion of the rest. To take one thing at a time is its normal principle. Whatever the field of interest, the mode of action is the same. If it selects a particular system, it tends to confine itself only to the working out of its principles unmindful of the existence of other alternatives and their possibilities. It is intensive but also exclusive. This is its normal feature.

But this does not work in life. That is why it is said life is larger than logic and the mind is obliged to compromise with the realities of life. Life is a field of several possibilities; it offers several options. The forces that operate in the field of life are never static. The very principle of life is movement, change, progress. The mind is more or less rigid in its beliefs and resists change. It is narrow in its range. Without the pressures of life, the mind would not move.

Life offers diversity, the mind prefers a selective unit to play with. Life teaches us to take cognisance of the several factors that are at work at different levels and we develop a practical intelligence—other than the logical mind—which knows how to compromise and coordinate the various elements for the maximum effect.

Ultimately it is in life that the truth or value of every science is tested. Mental constructions often break down when faced with the challenges of the intricacies of life. Life is complex, opulent, changing from moment to moment. Nature brings in the mind to introduce some order, coordination and harmony in the flux of the forces of life. The mind needs to be sufficiently plastic, ready to enlarge itself and extend its horrizons before it can hope to successfully fulfil the intention in Nature.

28-4-'88

96

LIBERATIONS

There is a strong tradition that liberation, *mukti*, is not complete till the body is shed. One may arrive, by strenuous discipline of yoga, at a state of union with the Self or the Divine. But this state is confined to the level of the soul, the inner being. One is not actively involved even when fulfilling one's responsibilities in life; as it is said, one may be in the world but yet not of the world.

In his inner life, his mental movements, emotions, vital responses he is aloof, not really touched by what goes on externally. He is aware that he is not the nature. He does not fight with its propensities. For he knows that his nature is bound to the past karma and to a certain extent to the karma that is being forged at present: all moves according to the relentless drive of his nature which is again subject to the gusts of universal nature. Nature has certain fixed habits which do not easily yield themselves to change. There is also the body-consciousness which identifies itself with and supports this habitual nature. To that extent he shares the bondage of nature. It is only when the body is shed and the nature—supported by the *samskāras* of the body—is dissolved, that he is truly free. This is known as *videha mukti*, liberation in the bodiless condition.

Spiritual experience, however, testifies to another state of liberation: *jivanmukti*, liberation while yet living. There is of course the central liberation in the Self or the Divine. The consciousness undergoes a radical change spiritually. But one does not stop with it. One follows it up by organising that freedom of the inner consciousness in the rest of the being. All movements of the outer being are turned into expressions of the inner state. The triple nature of mind, life and body is subjected to the action of the realised consciousness within. Corrective steps are taken to neutralise and eliminate as far as possible, the results of the past karma. In other words nature is not left to itself as incorrigible. It is disciplined and brought to participate in the liberated movements of the soul. Both within and without one is an integrated, liberated, being. He does not have to wait till death overtakes his body. He is liberated even while living, he is *jivan-mukta*.

What about the karma that is inescapable when one acts, as one has to, while living? All action proceeds from the level of the soul. One acts only under a divine impulsion; there is no personal motivation. External nature functions only as an instrumental agency and what it does under the direction of the liberated being, in a liberated, impersonal consciousness, does not bind. 30-4-'88

97

NIRVANA

Yogic nirvana is not an attainment, a siddhi that is built up gradually. It is a state that is suddenly realised when the personality of the individual falls off. As a result of the progressive thinning out of the ego, elimination of desire as a motivating agent in life, the outer person disappears from the scene. And there is a state of Nothingness. The individual who has been doing the sadhana is no longer there. All the attachments and personal formations have fallen off. The person constituted by them is also not there.

This is an experience that is most helpful in yoga. The separative personality is left behind. But on that account activity in life does not come to a stop. Though the personal centre of reference is no longer there, there is an automatic guidance on what is to be done at each moment. For this experience of Nirvana is not the ultimate goal in yoga. It is a stage to a greater realisation: the surface personality recedes and makes way for the revelation of the true individuality. This individuality, Sri Aurobindo points out, is other than the usual narrow, limited and limiting personality. It is something that is vast and infinite and capable of identifying itself with the whole world. True individuality is one with the world, contains the world in its consciousness.

This leads to further realisations. The individual realises identity with the One who is present in all. He experiences himself in all. He also realises his unity with the One who is manifest as the Many. The experience is not only of identity with an Omnipresence. He also realises the One as the Supreme Person, Purusha. All these multiple realisations of the true individual become possible because of the elimination of the separative surface individual self identified with nature—a fundamental step preceding the experience of Nirvana. Nirvana assures this freedom from the limitations of the provisional small external self and paves the way for larger and more fundamental realisations.
2-5-'88

98

'ORDINARY LIFE'

It is customary to refer to the daily life in the world with a deprecatory accent in spiritual circles. The implication is that this life is something undesirable from the higher standpoint of the seeker of spiritual values. It is perhaps inevitable as long as one is obliged to live amidst the society, but it is nevertheless a waste of time and energy, it has no real worth.

Actually life is what we make of it. Life is given to us as a field and an opportunity to grow in consciousness, enlarge ourselves, increase in knowledge, power and effectivity. It has a place of its own in the total scheme of the Reality in manifestation. It is in daily life that we learn—or rather should learn—to perfect ourselves, fulfil our deeper impulses, organise the circumstances to the utmost growth of ourselves and our fellowmen. That is why Sri Aurobindo says all life is yoga. Life itself must be turned into an essay in self-discipline and progressive self-development.

Indeed to live life well is not the end of things. It should be turned meaningful and preparatory to a higher life in which the lower finds its culmination. In other words our aim must be to exceed life, not reject or throw it away. The life that is given to us must be fully organised and lived to its optimum in terms of its intrinsic truths revealing the Divine Reality in the universe.

It is in this life that we learn to control and liberate ourselves from the hold of desire which is the main motive-force in the activities of life and mind. It is here that we learn to become conscious of the pseudo-self, the ego, around which our life in ignorance revolves. Nature delivers enough corrective shocks to expose this false centre of our existence. We are taught to subordinate it to the demands of our true self, the soul or psychic being, and eventually to thin it out. It is again through the disappointments, failures and helplessness in the maze of the forces of the world around us and within us, that we come to realise the basic limitations of our nature and learn to surrender to a Higher Power, the Divine, in order that the Higher Will may prevail and take over the reins of our life. These are the ways in which life teaches us to awake to the need of a truer life and helps us to convert our present existence into its higher term. Human life is a necessary step to divine life. Man must perfect his manhood before he is ready for godhood.

4-5-'88

99

HELL AND ITS POWERS

We no longer believe that there is a place called hell to which people who commit 'sin' are despatched after death. There is no such special location on the cosmic map. Hell is in fact a condition of mind, a state of being, which is full of unhappiness, misery, tension, pain, with no prospect of relief. External conditions have less to do with such a state than the inner conditions of a person.

Sri Aurobindo refers to four powers of hell which build up the state of hell. The first is obscurantism. It is a blind refusal to examine one's legacy of beliefs and attitudes in the light of growing knowledge. An obstinate sticking to irrational prejudices and primitive superstitions; resistance to enlightenment which may disturb the set-up of ignorance in which one is smugly stationed—these are the characteristic features of this retrograde opposition to progress—on any plane.

The next is falsehood. It is a conscious, deliberate twisting of fact with the intention of misleading. It is easy to enough to spot it in collective life when some elements indulge in it in order to misrepresent and misdirect the public mind. It can be combated with determination, though it may take time to do it effectively. It is more harmful when the individual harbours and indulges in falsehood. At first he may succeed with others and draw some advantage. But in the long run he finds himself a helpless victim to the habit of falsehood. The person is not conscious that he is speaking falsehood. He comes to believe in what he says: he suicides in a subtle way. Thus falsehood is deadly in its results.

The third power of hell is suffering. Suffering is more debilitating than pain. It is a psychological and emotional strain which drains away positive energies. The very balance of mind is struck and the person reacts to everything in a negative manner. Whatever the spiritual value of suffering when properly handled, the normal effect is one of demoralisation. Suffering saps at all will to redress and restore things to normalcy.

And the last is death. Death as it appears to the common mind, is the end of things. It is feared, sought to be avoided or at least put off as long as possible. Death implies decay and disintegration which by themselves cast a cold spell on the victim. He loses his will to survive and live. Pessimism colours his outlook and he becomes sour, bitter, thereby missing all the good that life offers.

These are the agents of hell. When any of them make their appearance it is time to be alert and stop them from weaving the net of hell around ourselves. The one sure and unfailing way to keep them out of our atmosphere is to awaken the psychic and increase its action in us.

5-5-'88

100

ATMOSPHERE

The Mother narrates how once in her early days she had called on a family which had just suffered a bereavement. It was more or less a formal call. But she soon found herself sobbing. She was surprised and on looking closely at herself she found that the grief in the atmosphere had affected her without her knowledge. This is just an instance how the atmosphere of a place plays an effective—though unseen—role in our life.

It is an inescapable experience in some holy centres to feel overwhelmed by feelings of devotion, an elevation in consciousness and a sense of purity. That is because the place has not only been sanctified by some highly endowed spiritual figure but also by the adoration and self-offering of countless pilgrims to the Deity of the spot. The reverse can also be true. Where the place has been filled with gross desires and remnants of religious bargains, the atmosphere is strongly vitiated and malevolent entities lodge themselves in the region causing untold hardships, accidents, strange illnesses etc. among the throngs of supplicants who flock to the place.

There are places like the cremation grounds where there is an understandable activity of departed spirits and similar formations of an eerie character. They are visited at odd hours by some men in order to gain certain occult powers from the denizens of the region. Unwary travellers passing by these places are likely to get unhappy experiences and consequent upsets in health.

And of course there are places where a powerful spiritual Presence presides. Invariably those who enter these premises experience an impact of peace, purity and quickening of aspiration for God. Even sceptics are known to have been overwhelmed by these spiritual charges in the atmosphere. Similarly there are atmospheres of learning, of health, of tapas—austerities—which preserve their character and potency for long. These atmospheres have not been formed in a day; a continuous effort has gone into the making of the special quality of the atmosphere.

There is something natural about these atmos-

pheres. This very innate quality steals into those who come into their environs and influence them even without their knowledge. Of course it is possible for one with a strong will to assert oneself and refuse to be touched by the negative elements in an atmosphere. But it is difficult to resist for long the effects of a strong spiritual atmosphere. The effects may not appear immediately; they may not do so even in the life-time. They touch the soul and the consequences may appear in a subsequent life.
6-5-'88

101

VAIRAGYA

It is not uncommon to see many leaders of action striking a defeatist note in the evening of their lives. They bemoan that they have wasted their efforts and the world being what it is nothing will ever improve. They give up. They declare the futility of attempts to change the order of things: nature will not change. And they turn to some contemplative type of life seeking relief elsewhere.

Usually this happens when men work for success. They have some ambition—however veiled—and when things do not work out as they had hoped for, they are overcome by frustration, heavy sense of failure. They recoil from life. If they do not turn exactly cynical they suffer from a strong dose of pessimism. They no longer believe in exerting themselves for the world. This kind of turning away from the call of duty, refusal to act one's part, is called tamasic *vairāgya*. Elements like inertia, lethargy, cover the mind and the vital. It is an indulgence in tamasic refusal to face life, not a genuine turning to the Divine. At the root is disappointment, failure, in one's efforts, not a true call to the higher dimensions of existence.

There is another kind of *vairāgya*, the sattwic. At some stage in life, one realises the puny nature of human capacities, the littleness of the ego-self, the shallowness of one's ideas, ideals and aims before the vastness of the Infinite Reality, the magnificance of the manifestation of God and the endless vistas of fulfilment that beckon the brave of spirit. This enlightenment of the mind results in a powerful fascination for a different order of life and at the same time an undue—and also untrue—devalution of the world. It often leads to an exaggerated view of the irreversibility of the limitations of human life and a reaction sets in. The extant negative features of earth-life come to be blown up and there is refusal to participate in it if one can help it.

In both these types of *vairāgya*, it may be noted, the urge to cease from exerting oneself in life here does not really come from the call of the soul to turn to the Divine. The inspiration is not truly spiritual. It is a reaction of the gunas of nature; there is either a disappointment or a sense of weakness, inadequacy, which makes the pendulum swing to an extreme of rejection of life and turn to spiritual interests. Often it happens that once the intensity of *vairāgya* wears off with the passage of time, the aspiration flags. It is also possible that the soul utilises some such debilitating experience in life as a spring board for its own journey homeward.
7-5-'88